Stardust and Scar Tissue

Stardust *and* Scar Tissue

*Ramblings, Ruminations,
and the Search for an
Authentic Culture of Life*

Mick Scott

OPINE
Press
WINSTON-SALEM, NORTH CAROLINA

OPINE PRESS
Press 53, LLC
PO Box 30314
Winston-Salem, NC 27130

First Edition

Cover design by Studio H
www.madebystudioh.com

Author photo by Andalnn Adele Addison

Library of Congress Control Number
2023947064

This book is a collection of previously published opinion columns
from the Winston-Salem Journal, written by Mick Scott from
April 28, 2016 to January 15, 2023, and reprinted with
permission from Lee Enterprises. To preserve these columns,
we followed the style guide of the Winston-Salem Journal,
which follows the AP Stylebook.

Opine Press is an imprint of Press 53.

ISBN 978-1-950413-71-3

Contents

How we got here

I started working at the Winston-Salem Journal, a storied newspaper I'd long admired, in 2000 as a part-time obituary clerk. I finished in 2023 as the Journal's editorial page editor. It was while serving on the editorial desk that I wrote these columns, my love letters to my city and state and its inhabitants, both tame and wild.

I have nothing but gratitude and affection for the Journal and those who have been associated with it over the years — its contributors, readers, supporters and critics. The Journal gave me a voice. I tried to give others a voice. We must have made a difference.

We made it, after all, together, through a deadly pandemic, through political turmoil and the demands of being adults in a confusing and turbulent world.

My thanks to Kevin Watson for encouraging and publishing this record of what I feel were my best efforts; to my mentors: Linda Brinson, Carl Crothers, John Railey and Allen Johnson; to my de facto editor and conscience, Cindy Hodnett; to my steadfast and supportive friends: Bob Beerman, Cyndi Briggs, Terri Kirby Erickson, Jack Hernon, and Eddie Huffman; and most of all, to my partner in foxology, Mary Dudley. I dedicate this book to Mary.

Secret treasures of the Inner Banks

Apr 28, 2016

U.S. Route 158 winds its way east from here, two lanes almost all the way to the coast. That's fine; I'm in no hurry.

I pass the ornate mustard Caswell County government building in Yanceyville, then through the one-street business districts of Oxford, Littleton and other spots on the road that take less than a minute to enter and exit.

Roanoke Rapids means it's time for a break, so I unload my bike and ride the up-and-down Roanoke Canal Trail. After a late lunch, it's back on the road, past the mysterious ruins by River Falls Park in Weldon ("Rockfish Capital of the World") and through another string of quaint old towns before eventually turning south on U.S. Route 17 to Elizabeth City. "Betty City," I call it, being an old friend.

This same highway provides access to other old friends: Hertford, Washington, Edenton, New Bern.

This is my vacation. And though I often travel to places I've never been — I've visited 49 of the 50 states and several out-of-country locations — I return to this part of the state, northeastern North Carolina, over and over, on average once a year. It resonates with me. It's not the Outer Banks, but the "Inner Banks," the coastal plain west of Pamlico Sound.

So much here appeals to me: The furrowed fields that push

the treeline back to the horizon. The midnight-dark skies. The laconic swamps, tannin-stained rivers and low-traffic towns with their hidden treasures. Like the abandoned but still ornate movie theater in the back of the hardware-appliance store in Hertford, or the riverside boardwalks leading nowhere in Windsor (the ones on the north side of town that you can't see from the road), or the Sans Souci cable ferry that crosses the Cashie River, where you honk your horn and the ferry master puts his coffee down and comes out of his house to pull you across.

There's not a lot to do on these trips but look and listen, and that's what I do, sitting in diners eavesdropping on old farmers swapping tales of weather and grown children or poking around second-hand bookstores and antique shops. It's not unusual to be noticed by people who are happy to see a new face. ("Hi there, where are you from?")

On occasion I'll turn north into the Virginia portion of the Great Dismal Swamp and bike to Lake Drummond, miles from any other human being but presumably close to thankfully shy bears. (*Meals on wheels*, I always think.)

Or I might visit one of the lush state parks like Merchants Millpond, where kayakers paddle near wary alligators, and Goose Creek, with a secret spot for stargazing, a local librarian revealed to me.

I often detour south to crystal-clear White Lake, pleasantly deserted in the off-season. Melvin's Diner, in nearby Elizabeth-town, serves tender cheeseburgers that I devour for every meal, including breakfast, when I'm in the area.

Usually on these trips I splurge a little bit, staying in local inns where I can converse with the owners. I walk the tightrope of reading small-town newspapers while trying to avoid politics. Sometimes it's difficult, like in 2013 when Belhaven residents were upset about the closing of the Vidant Pungo Hospital because of the legislature's refusal to expand Medicaid. (Belhaven Mayor Adam O'Neal walked to Washington, D.C., to protest, and now a new medical facility is scheduled to open in June.)

We hear how small towns are dying as their children and economic opportunities move to larger centers of commerce, and that's evident from the many dilapidated storefronts. But from time to time I still come across hip young people building community theaters or opening exotic restaurants or trying to find some other way to stay.

After dark I like the Edenton waterfront where the Chowan River pours into Swan Bay, and Union Point Park in New Bern, where the Trent and Neuese rivers meet and the headlights on the bridge crossing them look otherworldly.

Invariably I wonder what it would be like to live in this area. One friend, a lover of culture, thinks that without Aperture Cinema and Barnes & Noble to lean on, I would soon get bored. I've always had the notion that you can find what you want, no matter where you live, if you look for it.

But for now, I enjoy my brief glimpse into another place and another way of life. And when it's over, I'm happy to once again park my car in Winston-Salem.

Loretta Lynn sang for my mother

May 5, 2016

The thing that springs to mind about my mother, Ruby Geroline Vanhoy, who died almost three years ago, is that she loved to laugh and she loved to joke around.

During one of her final examinations, the doctor asked her, "Do you know what year it is?"

"It's 2013," she answered.

"And do you know where you are?"

"I'm right here!"

Mom was from good Winston-Salem country stock. She married young, lived to see grandchildren and great-grandchildren and she had the unwavering love and support of the best man I know, my father.

Mom also had a naturally cheerful disposition and a fun sense of humor. But in her early adulthood she began to experience problems. At times she was in bed for days, too depressed to function. At times she became paranoid and imagined unreal things. As a child, these incidents frightened me.

Mom was eventually diagnosed as having a chemical imbalance, and later still as bipolar. But people called it "nerves" back then and the treatments of the day only provided partial relief. Later, as treatments improved, she was able to cope well and function normally. But it was a painful process for her.

I didn't think about that while growing up. In fact, my attitude toward my mother wasn't very positive at all and I was often rude and disrespectful to her. Developmental psychologists tell us this is natural to some extent; all children reach the stage at which they feel the need to differentiate themselves from their parents and often do so by rebelling. But my disdain for my mother lasted far too long, into my adulthood. Objectively, I easily recognized Mom's good qualities, but I still constantly found fault in her.

Also, as an adult, I began to have my own bouts with depression and anxiety, which sometimes required professional treatment. Rather than make me more sympathetic to Mom's struggles, I resented her more, as if she were somehow responsible for my problems.

For years I thought that was just the way it was. Then something shifted.

During the last few years of her life, Mom's physical health deteriorated. She was confined to a wheelchair, had difficulty speaking and lost the ability to eat and sleep well. Her body shrank to a near skeleton. Her personality changed, too, and her temperament could be difficult, especially toward my father, who was her primary caregiver.

But while her body was exhausted, her spirit was tireless. She became more assertive, more gregarious, eager to be engaged in life. She would sit at a crowded dinner table, smiling and talking to the people around her, oblivious to the food.

During conversation, I might mention travel plans to her: "I'm going to Montana next month."

"Can I go with you?" she'd ask, only partly joking. She loved to travel and see new things. Dad often took her on day trips, and sometimes I'd join them, though the logistics of travel — too many moving parts — made it difficult. Still, she wanted to go somewhere, anywhere, all the time.

Through her tenacity, I came to respect her. She was a fighter; she wasn't going to give up easily. Her brittle and fragile skin became beautiful to me.

During her final few days, she lost lucidity, then consciousness. Eventually, one doctor told us that it was down to a matter of hours.

You don't know my mother, I thought.

She passed away in a hospice room with family and friends

gathered around. I found that I didn't feel sad when Mom died. I felt grateful that she'd had so much love in her life and that I'd finally found the grace to appreciate her.

When Loretta Lynn's new CD, "Full Circle," was released earlier this year, I bought a copy. Loretta was Mom's favorite singer; I think she found strength in Loretta's feisty songs like "You Ain't Woman Enough to Take My Man" and "Fist City." Just three months before Mom died, Dad and I took her, wheelchair and all, to hear Loretta sing at the Greensboro Coliseum.

One recent bright Saturday morning, I put "Full Circle" on the computer to listen to while I drank my coffee. On the fourth track, Loretta sang in her still-strong Kentucky voice, "Who's going to miss me? Who's going to miss me when I'm gone?"

I heard my mother's voice in the question. And through misty eyes, I answered the empty room.

"I will, Mom. I will."

The seeds that were planted at Morning Dew

Aug 25, 2016

I dropped into Coffee Park Arts for a cup and some tasty pumpkin bread recently and interrupted a conversation between co-owner Tommy Priest, pianist Damon Carmona and coffee roaster Nathan Smith.

"How can we get someone at the Journal to write about Morning Dew?" Tommy asked.

Well, I know a guy.

The Morning Dew Herb & Coffee Co. opened in a Burke Street storefront with a south-facing glass front, terra-cotta tile floors and sunny yellow walls on Feb. 24, 1995. The co-owners, Steve and Ginny Hunneke, were close friends of mine, and I worked behind the counter during the first few months it was open.

Morning Dew quickly became a social, artistic and cultural hub for Winston-Salem's loose Bohemian crowd. Poets, musicians, painters, painters' models, craftsmen, art students and teachers, kids and punks, along with people who read books and listened to music, gathered in its seats and on its sidewalk.

The "village elders," erudite painter Armand de Navarre and good-hearted art collector A.C. Dollar, were there most every morning, and others like Damon, Tommy and me joined them to drink our coffee, read the Journal and hold forth on matters of global import.

And we smoked. Oh my God, did we smoke.

In the evening, dozens would gather to flirt, laugh, gossip, play chess and, often, top off our caffeine levels before moving on to basement studios to practice our arts. Of course, we had our fair share of friction and drama, but for the most part, we were not just supportive, but *fans* of each others' work.

It was, for me, the most creative time of my young life. My friends and I put our canvasses on Morning Dew's walls and our poetry and musical performances on its stage.

It's hard for me to talk about that special time and place without worrying that I'll exaggerate. I'm tempted to compare it to the café society of 1920's Paris or the San Francisco Poetry Renaissance, which, in the light of day, feels like aggrandizing hyperbole. But just mentioning Morning Dew on Facebook last weekend generated enthusiastic responses that testify to its true significance.

My friend Nora Streed, who moved here from Minneapolis in 1996, wrote, "It was one of the places I visited, before I moved here, that made me say 'Yeah, I could live here. These are my people.' And they were. And are."

Restaurant maven Mary Haglund wrote, "I made muffins for Steve & Ginny that paid my rent$$. It was one of my first 'food gigs.' It gave me encouragement to dream about cooking for people."

Former Winston-Salem resident Mark Linga, now an arts educator at the List Visual Arts Center in Cambridge, said it best: "That amazing coffee shop was my spiritual home. It also inspired an entire generation of DIY free spirits to claim ownership of their cultural destiny. It was an incubator for numerous love affairs and friendships . . . a safe refuge for those gingerly making their way out in the world. It was an anchor for so many during a time when downtown W-S was literally a ghost town. It was an oasis for dreamers to dream big. Memories of Steve and Ginny and all of the artists, writers, musicians, free spirits live on in my heart. Nothing made Winston-Salem more amazing than that special place in that special time."

I don't think everybody gets to experience a place like Morning Dew. It wasn't by any means the only place we frequented, either; it was preceded and overlapped by the Rainbow News & Cafe, the Penny Universitie and other "third" places, and eventually followed by (anti)establishments like Krankies.

But there was something that set Morning Dew apart from the rest.

Walk through downtown Winston-Salem's Arts District and Innovation Quarter now and you'll find a wide variety of colorful cultural amenities, dining and entertainment venues interspersed with art galleries and working studios. Today's hipsters' experience of downtown is dramatically different from ours. Winston-Salem still has enough artistic talent for 10 cities its size, but with today's threatening tendencies toward social splintering and isolation, I fear the creative community lacks an unofficial clubhouse like ours to encourage friendship and collaboration.

Like all good things, Morning Dew couldn't last. It ended, not with a bang or a whimper, but with a series of bangs and whimpers, as some regulars moved away, to Boston or Los Angeles; some turned their attention to their young families; some vanished without a trace; some died. In 1999, Steve and Ginny sold Morning Dew and moved to Asheville. A couple of configurations later, it closed for good.

But by then, it had served its purpose as a springboard to other, richer destinations. Lee and Susan Terry, who met at the Dew, married and formed a unique musical partnership. Steve Wishnevsky builds bass guitars and manages the Winston-Salem Shuffle, a monthly talent showcase. Entrepreneur and urban pioneer John Bryan rebuilt half the city. Tommy and Kendall Priest own and operate Coffee Park while raising two lovely daughters. Mary Haglund opened her eponymous landmark restaurant.

Nathan Smith is building his own coffee-roasting business. Damon Carmona composes and arranges intricate songs and plays piano for the drama department at the UNC School of the Arts. Jack Hernon, the most authentic artist I know, still paints and works in the arts. He's still one of my closest friends.

Steve Hunneke, always so helpful to others, including me, died in 2006, a victim of long-term addictions. Armand and A.C. both died in 2007 after living full, successful lives. Ed Kinser also died in 2007, by his own hand. Eddie Rouse died of liver failure in 2014 after making a name for himself in Hollywood. We'll never forget them.

Ginny Hunneke, with her ever-present smile and easy

laugh, helped found a school in Asheville and is now the head conspirator at The Fun Conspiracy, a life-coaching and recovery organization that helps people find joy in their lives.

And me: I wound up reading and writing for a living.

Twenty-one years after it first opened, Tommy and Nathan are talking about a Morning Dew reunion, gathering the scattered members of the tribe once more to celebrate its legacy. If it happens — and it should — I hope it'll also serve, like Morning Dew did, to propel us forward.

Building the perfect beast

Sep 22, 2016

With the temperature more comfortable than it's been in months, I hoofed it to one of our city's lovely greenway trails after work last Friday. The sun was bright but not glaring and the air was full of sweet and earthy aromas. After passing a few other walkers and their gamboling dogs, I spotted, through the thick vegetation, the blue plastic of a tent or tarp and realized it must belong to someone with no better place to call home.

Not to diminish the challenges of the homeless, but I actually felt the tiniest twinge of envy at the thought of this home in the woods, where the air would soon cool, the breeze would rustle the leaves and the crickets could lullaby one to undisturbed sleep.

And I thought, as I so often do, why are things the way they are?

I don't mean why is the sky blue, or why is my skin getting wrinkly. More like: Why don't we all have tents in our backyards and sleep there on pleasant nights? Why do we chop down large shade trees and construct brick boxes into which we pump artificially cooled air and spend our evenings watching pretty people we'll never meet act out stories on electronic devices?

The eponymous heroine of Jamaica Kincaid's novel "Lucy," listening to a friend complain about the cold, asks, "How do you get to be a person who is made miserable because the weather changed its mind, because the weather doesn't live up to your expectations? How do you get to be that way?"

When the sky began to darken, I pulled out my telescope and set it toward the southeast, where the full moon would rise.

To some extent, our customs come about by accident. But they're also the result of thousands or possibly millions of decisions that were made independently but had interlocking pieces. We get used to them, are raised with them, and think they're just the way things are.

In the 1920s, the German government decided to standardize the size of office paper, Daniel Richards writes for the website Atlas Obscura. This led to standard sizes for books, desks and shelves — and eventually, boards and bricks. And though standardization was useful to the Nazi regime, it outlived their terrors to influence everything from the size of doors to the design of chicken coops. One system begat another and next thing you know, we can buy tangerines in January.

We read glorifying reports about the Scandinavians, who work less and vacation more, enjoying the benefits that we in America only assign the rich. Health care is affordable and universal. But despite fears of "socialism," they still have plenty of rich people and incentives and innovations. They've worked out a way to do it.

For decades, American productivity grew annually, even while salaries stagnated (though productivity now seems to be dropping, The Wall Street Journal reports). Social scientists warn us of the unhealthy dangers of overwork and stress. It's now a cliché that nobody on their death bed ever said, "I should have spent more time in the office." I think about James Taylor's poignant song "Millworker": "My life has been wasted, and I have been the fool/ to let this manufacturer use my body for a tool."

On Sunday, columnist Scott Sexton wrote about a woman who had to sue her insurance company to receive the benefits that the system was rigged to keep from her. We allow insurance companies to make billions in profits while denying us medicines and treatments we need, sometimes to survive.

How did it get to be this way?

I'm optimistic and think we'll find improvement in the future. But there seem to be many stumbles along the way.

My friend with teenagers who follows trends tells me that millennials aren't buying cars or houses. They see those things as a waste of money. They'd rather travel and have experiences with friends. Maybe they're onto something.

Eventually the moon peeked through the tree line, bright as a fire. For the next hour, I watched a visual orchestra as the moon rose, hovered and colored the black clouds pink and purple. The harvest moon, as it's called, filled my viewfinder with its flat, creamy mare and florescent highlands and the scattered debris of crater Tycho reaching for the horizon in every direction.

Most children who live in Winston-Salem have never seen the Milky Way. Why not? It's their birthright. They should be able to see it any night the sky is clear.

How do we get to be this way?

We get to be this way through one inattentive decision at a time.

A golden response to difficult situations

Oct 20, 2016

Gov. Pat McCrory has been treated horribly because of his support for HB2, he told a conservative group in Raleigh recently, as reported by The Charlotte Observer. He's been shunned by friends. He says he's received death threats.

It's disturbing to hear this. Though I may disagree with him on some issues, I don't think the governor is a bad egg. When I see and hear him on TV, he often seems earnest and capable. I was impressed by his gracious compliments to Roy Cooper at the end of their first debate earlier this month.

But while the governor and others try to minimize and define their resistance to LGBTQ rights as "a political disagreement," The Charlotte Observer followed its report on the governor's comments with stories of LGBTQ persecution in half of our state's 100 counties that include bullying — in at least once instance, leading to suicide — destruction of property and physical attacks.

I don't condone the rancor that's been aimed at McCrory, but I can understand it. It comes from a community that has historically been subject to persecution — bullied and beaten, fired from jobs, kicked out of homes, even murdered — for what most understand to be immutable characteristics. Even after they've proved their worth as contributing members of society, every incremental step toward acceptance and equality has been met by harsh resistance. HB2 was a legislative slap in the face and they don't want to put up with it anymore.

Some LGBTQ opponents have employed the political tactic of claiming that they're being discriminated against for exercising their "religious freedom" — essentially, the freedom to discriminate against others. It reminds me of the old pun, "Your honor, it all started when he hit me back."

A prominent conservative activist, Jesse Lee Peterson, employed this tactic on a widely viewed YouTube video in which he portrayed the customers involved in the Oregon bakery lawsuit, Laurel and Rachel Bowman-Cryer, as the instigators of the conflict, as if they had been scouring the Portland area, just aching to find someone to sue. The truth is that the couple had been longtime customers and friends of Aaron and Melissa Klein, co-owners of the now-closed Sweet Cakes by Melissa shop — or so they thought — the bakery that illegally turned them away. They were embarrassed and hurt and filed a complaint *in response.*

The situation soon escalated out of control, with both couples experiencing harassment that includes death threats.

And the situation has escalated out of control in North Carolina.

However one reads the Bible, the Gospels are pretty straight-forward, describing the teachings and ministry of Jesus. And the most significant moral teaching Jesus offered the world was what we've come to call "the Golden Rule." The principle didn't originate with Jesus — Confucius and other philosophers were stating much the same thing long before his birth — but Jesus articulated it in a way that has resonated through the ages: "Do unto others as you would have them do unto you."

One has to assume that Jesus wasn't instructing his followers to be nice to the people with whom they already agreed. There would be no need to say that. He also wasn't telling them to get in other people's faces and straighten them out — the "I would *want* someone to tell me if I was doing wrong" spin. No encouragement is needed to spur that human instinct.

Jesus was telling his followers to respect — and treat well — even those with whom they disagreed.

It's an attitude that echoes throughout the Gospels. A

companion passage has Jesus telling his followers, "If a man compels you to walk one mile with him" — a right that the Romans of the day exercised against the people they conquered — "walk two."

How is that *not* the universal Christian response?

Some Christians will always condemn homosexuality, and they have that right. As generous as I can be, though, I can't see how that conviction becomes a legitimate excuse to override Christianity's prime directive: Treat them the way you want to be treated.

But for those who won't, it's hard to muster much sympathy when they are treated as they have chosen to treat others.

Seeking shelter from the storm

Dec 8, 2016

Have you heard the one about the man sitting on top of his house after a flood?

A boat approaches and its skipper invites the man to ride along to safety.

"No, thanks," the man replies. "I'm waiting for God to save me."

Another boat approaches and the same offer receives the same reply.

A helicopter pauses and drops a ladder.

"No, thanks. I'm waiting for God to save me."

The waters rise and the man drowns. In the hereafter, he approaches the throne and can't help himself:

"God, why did you let me drown? I was waiting for you to save me!"

The Almighty replies: "I sent you two boats and a helicopter, whaddya want?"

The old joke crossed my mind last week as I vacationed in the Bertie County town of Windsor. It was inundated by rising flood waters from the Cashie River after Hurricane Matthew in September, but the waters have now receded. The alpaca, zebra and emu have been returned to the mini-zoo and the quiet boardwalk leading to the river, a kayaker's paradise, looks none the worse for submersion.

But several businesses remain closed in Windsor, some for good. The inundated library has been stripped bare of books and shelves. And this may have been my last stay in the town's only inn, a warm and comfortable oasis. After four floods in 10 years, the owner says she's had enough and will sell the inn or auction off its effects next year.

The 2013 documentary "If You Build It" portrays Bertie County as struggling, not only with poverty and an obscenely dysfunctional educational system, but with a local leadership structure that fears relinquishing power to "outsiders." An acquaintance in town confirmed this analysis and cited high-schoolers who have never been taught how to multiply and divide or, in some cases, even how to endorse checks.

The joke also crossed my mind on election night, as I followed the returns with anchor Katie Couric and her panel of Washington insiders on Yahoo News. One of her guests was Bo Copley, a plain-spoken, unemployed coal miner from West Virginia who received media attention earlier this year after passionately advocating for his state, his family and his livelihood to candidate Hillary Clinton.

Referring to his year-long unemployment, Couric asked Copley if he had considered government-subsidized retraining programs to help him learn new skills.

"I feel like I'm led by the Lord and I want to do what he wants me to do," Copley responded, "so we're kind of just waiting on him to point me in the right direction, then we'll pursue those avenues once we know that we're going in the direction that he wants us to go in."

Bo. Buddy. The Lord sent you two boats . . .

But change is hard, especially when your job fits and your children are happy where they live. Change is hard in a state like North Carolina, where sharply curtailed benefits often don't allow the unemployed the leisure to wait for the Lord's guidance.

I drove south to "Little Washington" and strolled past busy art galleries and coffee shops before standing in line at Bill's Hot Dogs to get two (all the way but onions). I took my lunch to a bench on the northern bank of the Pamlico River, watching the boats sway and the sunshine sparkle in the water. Foot traffic was vigorous. City employees with brushes and rollers freshened up the vibrant blue paint on the rails by the riverwalk. There had been some flooding, I was told, but it did little damage and receded quickly.

An earworm kept repeating the lines from a 1984 Springsteen song:

> *They're closing down the textile mill*
> *across the railroad tracks*
> *Foreman says these jobs are going,*
> *boys, and they ain't coming back*

President-elect Donald Trump has promised to bring those jobs back, though, along with a former social order.

As I drove toward Southport, I heard on the radio Trump's claim to have saved 1,000 Indiana manufacturing jobs at the bargain price of $7 million. I later learned that Indiana manufacturer Carrier offers employees a generous, four-year re-education program "to develop new skills in a field of their choice," reporter Ethan Wolff-Mann wrote for Yahoo Finance. The program has awarded 38,000 degrees since 1996 and currently has 7,000 enrolled.

I spent the night in Southport before hiking in the Nature Conservancy's lush Green Swamp Preserve — a story for another day — then heading for home.

I asked a friend, an economist who lives in the area, what's the difference between Windsor, deadlocked in poverty and dysfunction, and Washington, which seems to be thriving?

"Washington has a plan," he told me. "Windsor doesn't."

Washington leaders have committed to recruiting new businesses and industry. They decided to listen. To diversify their economic base. To invest. To let outsiders in. To sail toward a bright future rather than cling to a stagnant past.

They took the boat.

What would Captain America do?

Feb. 23, 2017

It all began in 1965 with show and tell.

One of my first-grade classmates brought his prized possession to school, a book full of pictures of super-powered teenagers in colorful costumes. They could shoot power rays from their hands, or turn invisible, or fly!

When I got home, I gushed about it to my parents — "it's called a comic book!" — and asked them if I could get some.

Later, at the register at Chuck's Curb Market, my dad was firm: "Now, this isn't going to be a habit."

But I already knew that it would be. Because I had fallen in love. I fell in love with comic books and I've loved them ever since.

I loved the sheer pageantry of them, with lurid illustrations of heroes and villains in bold primary colors. I loved the sci-fi ray guns and spaceships and creepy monsters, reaching for me from the page with their wiggly tentacles.

Most kids in the 1960s read a few random issues of Superman and The Hulk before sports or the opposite sex captured their attention. But at the point when I might have normally aged out, comics companies tried to retain their readers with more complex characters and sophisticated story lines. I stuck around to read about some of the more pressing issues of the day: Prejudice. Drugs. Discotheques.

My favorite characters included the Batman, of course, as well as Nick Fury, Agent of S.H.I.E.L.D. and the Green Arrow. But I admired no hero more than Captain America, who was somehow able to deliver scathing lectures about freedom and justice while pummeling the Red Skull with his fists.

At some point I realized that actual human beings made these books. I began to recognize the expressive styles of various creators and could reel off the names of my favorite artists and writers like baseball fans would their favorite team's roster. These creators became my heroes, too.

I made friends with other fans and attended conventions where we met the creators. I bought special boxes and bags in which to store and preserve my books. But though I might have justified my hobby with the pretense that the books would one day be valuable, the most important aspect was always the experience of reading them.

For a small, shy misfit who suffered his fair share of bullying, comic books were a lifeline that provided a social, artistic and intellectual outlet. As cartoonist Tom Batiuk's "Funky Winkerbean" character "Crazy Harry" put it: "They did what superheroes are supposed to do. They saved me."

Over time, while I was being entertained, the books imparted another gift: values.

Fantagraphics Books editor Brian M. Kane expressed this idea last year while writing about the Sunday comics character Prince Valiant: "Val has a code of honor, which speaks to helping the weak and oppressed, to seeing the good in people — especially those who are different from us, to bringing the wrong-doers to justice, and to standing up for what is right even when the odds are against you. . . . Val presented a moral template for heroes who fought against ignorance and oppression as beacons of hope."

Stan Lee, Marvel Comics publisher and World War II veteran, inscribed his character Spider-Man with an unparalleled code: "With great power comes great responsibility." In 1970, Lee explained why it was important for his comics to deal with morality:

"None of us lives in a vacuum — none of us is untouched by the everyday events about us — events which shape our stories just as they shape our lives. Sure our tales can be called escapist

— but just because something's for fun, doesn't mean we have to blanket our brains while we read it!"

Through comic books and their heroes, I learned about fairness, integrity, determination and courage. I learned about internal struggles to defeat selfishness, prejudice and pride. I learned that you don't punch down. These are human values, unique to no particular philosophy, religion or political persuasion. They are measures of decency.

Life today is complex, with multi-faceted concerns and the compromises of adulthood. But I still find nobility and inspiration from my heroes. If you look for it, you can, too.

Stand for what's right even when the odds are against you. Be honest and be fair. And don't punch down.

Leaping free from the world's nets

Mar 18, 2018

An optimist is a man who takes his sunglasses with him on a cloudy day. So, being fairly optimistic, I was prepared two Saturdays ago for the few minutes that the sun lit the otherwise-overcast sky while I was strolling through Quarry Park.

The park opened last August and is still something of an undiscovered gem. I go there when I could use some fresh air and a clear head. And while the observation pier stretching above the quarry itself is the focal point for many, the paths leading away from the quarry are equally appealing to me. (It helps that the walkways from the parking lot curve around, rather than going straight to the pier, as if to say, *slow down, now, no need to rush*. Good job, city planners.)

I sometimes begin with the walkway leading downward, north, linking the park to the Peachtree Greenway, pausing at the various observation points to get a different perspective. Sometimes when I've felt energetic, I've started my walk at Winston-Salem State University and hiked up the hill to the quarry. Whew.

But it's the Waughtown Connector on the south side, stretching through the woods past Leight Street, that I enjoy the most. I've walked it in the spring, with the wind playing the leaves and swaying the oaks, maples and pines; in the fall, with blazingly bright leaves and broken branches coating the asphalt trail and the skeleton limbs of trees reaching into the sky; and in the winter, bundled up, peeking into the woods for the deer that forage there.

Often in the winter I've been reminded of the ninth-century Chinese poet Han-shan — whose self-appointed name means "Cold Mountain" to represent his hermitage — and his words:

> *I'm on the trail to Cold Mountain.*
> *Cold Mountain trail never ends.*
> *Long clefts thick with rock and stones,*
> *Wide streams buried in dense grass.*
> *Slippery moss, but there's been no rain,*
> *Pine trees sigh, but there's no wind.*
> *Who can leap the world's net,*
> *Sit here in the white clouds with me?*

Close to Marble Street, someone has tagged the asphalt: SOUTH 1800 BLOXK. When I first read those words, I thought, *yes, take ownership of the park, like I have.*

Eventually, I reach the modern steel observation pier, looking down 100-foot cliffs to the 12-acre pool below, with the Winston-Salem skyline in the distance. The granite walls of the quarry are gray, black, rust, ochre, yellow; the water, depending on the sky, can be a brilliant blue, pearl gray or black.

Though I enjoy solitary times at the park — early mornings and evenings, mostly — I also appreciate seeing others there. Knowing that the park is supported means it's more likely to be well tended and perhaps expanded. I typically see young couples, older couples, groups of teenagers, kids on bikes and scooters. Their relaxed smiles and quiet conversations indicated that they appreciated the park, too.

Quarry Park walks are one aspect of a multifaceted practice to deal with the stress and pressures of modern-day life. I'm aggressive about relaxation.

I realize the oxymoron there.

But I've known too many people who weren't. I've seen the effects of stress on friends and acquaintances.

Debilitating stress isn't always the result of one cataclysmic event; it can accumulate in increments, over time. Medical authorities warn us of high blood pressure and intestinal difficulties, anxiety and depression or worse.

Molecule by molecule, the little things can add up, almost unnoticed, until all of a sudden, one wonders how life suddenly became so grim.

But stress can be fought the same way: in increments, molecule by molecule. A walk in the park, an hour's exercise, a visit to a favorite bookstore, an evening with friends ...

And honestly; couldn't we all use a breather? A little time away from screens?

When plans were first being discussed for Quarry Park, there was talk of amenities like an amphitheater and a train running around the top of the quarry. The ideas seemed exciting on paper, but now I hope city planners will proceed with restraint. Quarry Park is an eminently relaxing park, with its trails, its open, spacious fields and its distance from noise and bustle. It should retain that character.

So if you're ready for a little relaxation, I've got just the place for you.

> *Who can leap the world's net,*
> *Sit here above the quarry with me?*

Ode to a piece of wood

Feb 24, 2019

It's just a stick.

A walking stick, to be precise, it was a Christmas gift I bought for myself from a curiosity shop downtown. I didn't need a walking stick, but something about it caught my eye and when I picked it up, it felt good. There was a gentle curve to it. It was light but strong.

I left it there at first, thinking it would be a frivolous purchase, but finally couldn't resist it any longer and went back for it. I pictured myself swinging it and tapping it on the ground along the trails at Quarry Park during my early morning walks.

There's nothing fancy about it; no metal or stones attached, no lacquer applied to make it shine. It was actually a little rough and I had to sand it a bit to make it comfortable.

The one detail is some Japanese script carved into it. A friend who knows Japanese translated parts of it: "Arizona." "17."

There's a story in there somewhere.

I showed it to another friend who is a luthier and he was unable to identify the type of wood from which the stick is carved. Possibly mahogany.

I took it to the park with me and as I began my walk, it fell out of my hand, again and again. I had to laugh. At just under 38 inches, it was too short and slid out of my hand on the outward swing.

Since then I've adjusted a little and it's all right. Even at home, I keep it at hand. Sometimes I just hold it and look at its grain. It's warm to the touch.

It's strange, the things that capture our attention, the things in which we see beauty.

There's a whole science of aesthetics that quantifies qualities like color, proportion and texture to explain why some things appeal to our senses. Learning aesthetics can enhance our perception of the world around us: architecture, gardens, fashion, book design. But at some point, we just like what we like. *Somebody* buys those velvet pictures of kittens with big eyes.

Many people have that kind of reaction to music. The finest moment of Bruce Willis' acting career may be in the 1995 sci-fi film "12 Monkeys" when, as a man from a bleak future, he tears up and smiles while listening to a recording of Fats Domino singing "Blueberry Hill."

In "In Praise of Shadows," Junichiro Tanizaki writes about the aesthetic choices applied to the design of objects like paper and tableware and the difference they make in the experiencing of them. Writing of Japanese pottery, he says, "We do not dislike everything that shines, but we do prefer a pensive luster to a shallow brilliance, a murky light that, whether in a stone or an artifact, bespeaks a sheen of antiquity." He describes a gentle glow "that comes of being touched over and over again, a sheen produced by the oils that naturally permeate an object over long years of handling . . ."

"Beauty is truth, truth beauty," John Keats memorably wrote in "Ode to a Grecian Urn." For a long time I considered that phrase to be frilly poetry with no real meaning. But I finally realized that beauty *is* truth — the truth of ourselves, of what we value.

Beauty is refreshing. It resonates within us, often producing a sort of deep sigh of relief.

Of course, beauty can lie, too, taking us down beguiling pathways of self-satisfaction and pride that are ultimately detrimental to our well-being.

I suspect we can tell whether beauty is speaking honestly to us by the results of our reaction — whether we become more generous in spirit or less so.

Are there political implications to beauty? Well, it would be a stretch to say that the Constitution promises us life, liberty and the pursuit of beauty, but it's just about there. It's the beauty we find in life, along with the liberty to pursue it, that makes it worth living, that keeps life from being drudgery, a repetition of work, rest, work, rest.

It's the beauty in simple things, like a well-crafted tool, the late-day sun shining on red bricks, a scattering of rocks, or in art and music, in special people, that makes it all worth living.

Without it, life is bereft.

Living in the City of Arts and Innovation puts us in the company of people who create beauty of all sorts. As my stick and I crossed Quarry Park, we found that someone had taken fresh spray paint to the asphalt of the Waughtown Connector, leaving several wavy and squiggly lines. At the risk of encouraging vandalism — which would just be *wrong* — I have to say that I saw it as a gift of beauty. I like the intentional pattern of the lines. I like their unexpected presence. I hope others find it pleasing, too, including the anonymous artist.

We are stardust and scar tissue

Mar 10, 2019

It was about a year ago, on a drier and warmer spring day, that she who brightens my days and I took our cameras in search of Winston-Salem wabi-sabi.

We figured we'd have some luck around the Innovation Quarter, with its repurposed buildings and R.J. Reynolds smokestacks, so we parked near the head of the Long Branch Trail and roamed.

During the course of a couple of hours, we photographed weathered wood, cracked brick and stained concrete. Probably the score of the day was a few shots of rust-colored stone under the railroad track that crosses East Fourth Street, where the year "1944" is engraved. Our photos will never be in a museum, but we enjoy looking at them every now and then.

"Wabi-sabi" is a Japanese term that doesn't lend itself to easy translation, and I can't pretend to have mastered it, but essentially it refers to finding aesthetic beauty in imperfection. It carries a connotation of impermanence and decay.

And though it's a principle most often applied to objects — the rusted steel of a railroad bridge; colorful paint peeling from a wall; spider-web cracks in porcelain — it's also intended to apply to the transience and flaws to be found in life itself.

"In the 14th Century," writes Jack Richardson in "Wabi-Sabi

and Understanding Japan," "wabi-sabi began to imply rustic simplicity in a positive light, or the grace that comes with age and use."

Some mornings when it's cool, my left ankle is stiff and I limp a little, a souvenir of an accident some 15 years ago. I look in the mirror and see bags under my eyes, maybe a new facial blemish. I've begun to think of this as my own experience of wabi-sabi. We humans are, after all, about as impermanent as things come. The best of us take it all in stride, with humor and grace.

Comedienne/writer Pamela Adlon did so recently when she talked to Terry Gross of "Fresh Air" about the power of accepting her age (52): "When you get comfortable with yourself, it's a way of feeling confident. . . . You look in the mirror and you're like, 'Oh, I guess this is my neck now. OK. Well, let's keep going with that.'"

And it's not just our physical bodies that change over time. The years also visit us with psychic and emotional burdens, the wear and tear of life's disappointments.

As they accumulate, they, too, offer their own use and grace, if handled well. When that imminent philosopher, Captain James T. Kirk, in "Star Trek V: The Final Frontier," is offered transcendental relief from his emotional burdens, he replies, ". . . pain and guilt can't be taken away with the wave of a magic wand. They're the things we carry with us, the things that make us who we are. If we lose them, we lose ourselves. I don't want my pain taken away, I need my pain."

Often our pains teach us mercy and compassion.

If not handled well, they can lead to cruelty and fear.

Nations, too, suffer the accumulation of time. In the state of Texas, a battle has raged for years over the content of American history books. (Because of its size, the standards set there are often applied across the country.) A conservative faction has been spearheading an organized effort to sanitize our history of some of its worst episodes, from the breaking of treaties with Native Americans to slavery, America's original sin. They also seek to minimize civil rights struggles and minority contributions. They went so far in 2015 as to have history books describe slaves as "workers" who had migrated here from Africa.

I think I understand their motive, at least in part: They want to present a portrait of America in which their children can take pride.

And well they should. America is a nation of great achievements. We've collectively created communities of prosperity. We've built an interstate highway system that allows commerce to cross the continent and a national parks system that preserves natural beauty for future generations. We were essential to ending Hitler's reign of terror. We've sent men to the moon.

But denying our nation's flaws would do our children a disservice. It would turn education into indoctrination. Not only would it create a false narrative, but it sets the stage for disillusion when students finally learn the truth — that America isn't perfect.

Our struggles to achieve a more perfect union, to find justice for all rather than boost privilege for a few — these are indispensable parts of the American story. They make us who we are.

Our nation's flaws don't make us beautiful. But denying them makes us ugly.

Bigfoot is alive and well
and living in the Tar Heel state

May 5, 2019

They say he stinks, but I don't care. I love Bigfoot.

There; I said it.

Not that I've ever met him, her or them. But others say they have. Hundreds of thousands claim to have seen, smelled, heard, maybe even spent a weekend with one of these reclusive, hairy, odoriferous giants.

And like other enthusiasms that have stuck with me since I was 12 — comic books, caverns, space exploration — I keep an ear perked for news of the elusive yeti, Sasquatch, skunk ape.

So it was I found myself in Littleton, a tiny town of about 600 residents a bit west of Roanoke Rapids, two weekends ago for the first annual Crypto Paranormal Festival, where Bigfoot was the motif of the day. The festival was held at the Lakeland Cultural Arts Center, a former high school auditorium that has found new life as a volunteer-run community theater and events center.

The program began with a couple of locals — one a school teacher, the other a trucker — sharing their eyewitness accounts of chance observations of something crossing their line of vision — something that, by process of elimination, *had* to be Bigfoot.

The keynote address came from Ken Gerhard, a professional cryptozoologist — someone who studies animals whose existence is unsubstantiated — who has appeared widely on TV. He admitted up front that he'd never seen a Bigfoot, but had heard hundreds of stories from those who have. And Gerhard had a cellphone recording of an eerie-sounding howl that, by process of elimination, *had* to be Bigfoot.

Between presentations, I wandered through the merchandise room, where the speakers and others sold wares that included food, books, soap and jewelry, much of which had a Bigfoot theme. During a break for lunch, I spoke with a couple of retirees from nearby Lake Gaston who perform in local community theater as we listened to a young musician play, artfully, an out-of-tune piano. I also met and talked with Stephen Barcelo, the open, friendly man behind all of this activity. A former photographer from New Jersey, he moved to Littleton around 2013 and, before long, began hearing stories. Residents sporadically see not only Bigfoot, but other mysterious creatures in the woods. One thing led to another and Barcelo now has a new career as the proprietor of the town's Cryptozoological and Paranormal Museum, as well as a seat on the town council. His advocacy has brought a considerable amount of media attention and commerce to Littleton.

I spent other parts of the weekend in neighboring Warrenton, a small-town enclave for well-to-do retirees, where I strolled past Antebellum and Craftsman-style houses decorated with roses and azaleas. I had dinner at the highly recommended Burger Barn.

For the record, I'm skeptical when it comes to Bigfoot. Somehow, despite all the eyewitnesses, the evidence hasn't yet met the stringent requirements of the scientific, legislative or journalistic communities.

But I love the stories. I love imagining Bigfoot tromping around the forests and mountains, the "undisputed hide-and-seek world champion," as one bumper sticker at the festival put it, avoiding, whether through shyness or disgust, the corrupting influence of mankind. I love the thought, as I've written before, that something wild exists out there, beyond our control.

And I like that Bigfoot sightings are democratic — he doesn't reveal himself to a preferred audience. Anyone might catch a glimpse.

Everyone I spoke to at the festival was friendly and cheerful.

Nobody argued or fought. Nobody signaled any interest in politics or religion. It was all about Biggie.

"The mystery is what is fun about it," Sarah McCann, a docent in a cryptozoology museum in Portland, Maine, told NBC's LiveScience a few years ago. "There will always be mysteries out there. Whether or not Bigfoot is real doesn't matter terribly."

Unlike so many other topics that require our attention.

In the paranormal museum, I studied a map that marked Bigfoot sightings in the state. Large clusters of pins were stuck in the Blue Ridge and Uwharrie mountains, and some along the coast — and quite a few in Littleton — but Bigfoot seems reluctant to enter the Piedmont.

What do we have to do to lure him?

There seemed to be something in the woods in Mocksville a few months ago, with glowing red eyes, that prompted calls to the Davie County Animal Shelter. But that turned out to be an 8-foot-tall statue some witty provocateur had placed in the woods on his property.

As the weekend waned, I drove back to Winston-Salem via the two lanes of U.S. 158, pausing in Henderson for homemade biscuits and Yanceyville to watch a fountain bubble in the Caswell County Arboretum. No Bigfoot followed me home. As far as I know.

It's not as simple
as black and white

Jun 2, 2019

I've always admired people who can think on their toes, who can see through the clutter of confusion, cut the BS and say what's what.

I'm not like that at all. A slow (but deep, I hope) thinker, I often have to mull things over when presented with the unfamiliar or unexpected. "Let me sleep on it" — that should be my motto.

Thus it was a couple of weeks ago when I received a phone call that baffled me. The caller, in brief, wanted to know, "Why is it that they can put up a statue of Martin Luther King for the blacks, but you can't have a Confederate statue for the whites?"

My reply was ". . ."

Then I added, "Ma'am, you've rendered me speechless. I don't think those are the same things, but I honestly don't know how to reply to you right now." (In my defense, I was concentrating hard on something else at the time. Plus, I'm not the Civil Rights AskSAM; what I don't know fills volumes.)

But it didn't take long after getting off the phone to realize that the confusion was in the question itself.

Is a Confederate statue really "for the whites"? If so, that negates the argument that such statues don't represent white supremacy.

Which isn't a surprise. Some look at such statues and see symbols of some mystical "heritage" that is worthy of honor. But I'm among those to whom such statues are so closely identified with the false, nation-dividing philosophy of white supremacy — as well defined in so many Articles of Confederation — that I want nothing to do with them. I know many other white folks who feel the same way. No, that statue's not for me.

And is a statue of civil rights icon Martin Luther King "for the blacks"? I'd think it would be for anyone who believes in fairness and justice. After all, King didn't promote black supremacy — he advocated for equality. His whole ministry was against the segregation and racial discrimination that was so prevalent at the time. He wanted blacks and whites to walk together in harmony.

On his memorial in Washington D.C., among other quotes, you'll find engraved, "Darkness cannot drive out darkness, only light can do that. Hate cannot drive out hate, only love can do that." Good people can agree to that no matter their race.

You won't find such statements engraved on a Confederate statue.

Content matters. There's a distinct difference between a statue honoring racial supremacy and a statue honoring racial equality and, to me, that's a much more important distinction than the skin color of the figure covered in bronze.

Beyond that, the question was troublesome because it hinted at a sort of victimization; her premise was that blacks were getting something that whites aren't allowed. (Because you just don't see statues of white people anywhere.)

A person of any race can be bigoted, of course, but storehouses of data tell us that blacks in America more often wind up being treated with discriminatory intent than whites, even today when institutionalized segregation has been so diminished. Google "living while black" and you'll find numerous incidents of African Americans whose mere presence in public is challenged — and who sometimes have the police called on them — while simply minding their own business: barbecuing in a park, working out in a gym, dozing off in a college common room (an enrolled student), mowing a lawn, entering their own homes, waiting for a friend at Starbucks (which received a lot of national attention) and other common activities. Where white people are regularly ignored, suspicion accompanies our black neighbors. To pretend that blacks are conferred some special privilege because of their color is absurd.

But I know my caller isn't alone; there are forces at work today that are victimizing white people by *telling* them that they're being victimized by minorities. These forces get away with it because they know how to manipulate information and because, as some wise person said, when you're accustomed to privilege, equality feels like oppression. When you're used to a compliant underclass, seeing its members making strides, being treated with acceptance rather than scorn, can be difficult to comprehend and accept.

But it's necessary to do so.

As is so often the case, the cure for ignorance is education. But there's no formal course; each of us has to take responsibility for the voices we're listening to and determine whether they're encouraging discrimination and victimization or wisdom and kindness.

To my friend, the caller, let me have a do-over. To some degree, we all get to choose how we look at life. Let me suggest trying to see things from a different perspective. Literally seeing only black and white is way too simplistic. There's a bright, colorful world out there, and those who refuse to see it may as well be blind.

Take me to the place I love

Jul 28, 2019

There's a crucial scene in the beautiful and poignant film "The Last Black Man in San Francisco" in which — spoiler alert — the protagonist, Jimmie Fails, is sitting on a city bus listening to a couple of transplants complain at length about how Frisco just wasn't what they imagined it would be. "The city's dead," one intones.

Fails, facing his own disappointments with the city, interrupts their diatribe: "'Scuse me. You don't get to hate San Francisco."

They object. "Sorry, but I'll hate what I want," one says.

"Do you love it?" he asks.

"It's — I mean, yeah, I'm here, but do I have to *love* it?"

"You don't get to hate it unless you love it," Jimmie replies. And things get quiet.

This segment, along with a few others, stuck with me for days. I wandered around town, hearing the movie's soundtrack in my head and looking for opportunities to dramatically say to someone: "You don't get to hate Winston-Salem unless you love Winston-Salem."

They never materialized. Probably for the best.

At the risk of ruining the poetry of the line, its meaning is clear: You don't have a right to criticize unless you've committed yourself to the thing you're criticizing. Only when you truly know it do you get a say. It's a sentiment I've heard from military veterans, who hear plenty of criticism of something they love from people who never served.

I wouldn't say this applies 100% of the time, of course; sometimes an outsider's objective perspective can teach us something important, even essential. But experience and commitment certainly lend weight to criticism.

I've written before about my return to Winston-Salem — the town of my birth — in 1988, which marked for me the beginning of my social and creative life as an adult. I invested myself, forming friendships and habits that have lasted to this day.

It hasn't always been smooth. This city has, at times, driven me crazy. There've been times when I've felt like a restless teenager fed up with his stupid parents.

But I love it. I feel proud when I walk through its downtown and its parks. I feel proud of the people I know here, my friends and acquaintances, kind people and quirky malcontents, their talent, humor and skills, their manners and compassion. We have so much beauty.

Every now and then after I moved here, I'd meet someone who came for work or family but longed to get out. "There's nothing to do here," they'd tell me, along with other complaints.

I'd often respond by introducing them to my friends. I'd invite them to parties and events. Sometimes, my friends became theirs. Sometimes, they found their footing and made this their home.

But sometimes, as they continued to moan, I'd just get fed up with them. You don't get to hate it unless you love it.

After seeing "Last Black Man," a couple of things happened in the world. One was that the New York Times offered a sober-eyed assessment of Winston-Salem that raised a few hackles — and served as a reminder that we're not perfect. Fair enough.

Another is that President Trump told some Democratic representatives, American women of color — "the Squad" — that they didn't belong here and should go back to their own countries. Pressed to explain, he accused them of hating America.

"They have to love our country," Trump said.

It would seem an echo of Fails's statement, and you might think it would resonate with me.

But the real reason for Trump's complaint was pretty transparent, as it usually is. It was Trump they didn't love. As for America . . .

Those people I used to know who said, "There's nothing to do here"? I don't see them anymore. They didn't buy houses. They didn't run for office. They didn't like it, so they left.

But the Squad, they didn't leave. Instead, they invested themselves.

James Baldwin, in "Notes of a Native Son," wrote, "I love America more than any other country in this world, and, exactly for this reason, I insist on the right to criticize her perpetually."

Me, too.

There are things about this nation that shame me, that anger me, many of them related to a pervasive cultural insistence on monetizing everything. From clean air and water to health care to education, someone is always asking, *how much is it going to cost me to do the right thing?* And we accept that as not just legitimate, but admirable. We allow some people to storehouse their wealth while helpless people go hungry. One doesn't have to be a socialist to say that something is wrong with that system.

I get to say those things. And so do you.

You don't need a weatherman

Aug 11, 2019

I first began reading the Bible for myself when I was a teenager — an exercise I would recommend to anyone, for a variety of reasons — and in the Gospel of Luke, I came across what is sometimes called the Parable of the Shrewd Manager.

In a nutshell, it's the story of a business manager who realizes he's in trouble with his boss and likely to be fired. So he goes to merchants who owe his boss money and cuts their debt. He does this so that when he loses his job, "people will welcome me into their houses." Jesus commends the manager's shrewdness.

The story didn't make much sense to me at the time. At 16, I wondered why Jesus would praise someone who cheated his own boss. I didn't understand then that debt is negotiable.

But I eventually got the deeper lesson, which is that the manager knew which way the wind was blowing and took steps to prepare what you might call a soft landing. Shrewd, indeed.

I thought about that parable recently while talking with a friend who is Hispanic — an accomplished businessman from an accomplished family who has contributed greatly to our community. Among other things, we discussed the unstoppable demographic changes occurring in America. By 2050, the U.S. Census Bureau reports, current minorities will make up more than 50 percent of the population and whites will essentially be a minority. We're both dismayed at the "racial anxiety" — to be overly polite — that this change seems to elicit in some segments of the white population — and how that anxiety has been manipulated by a lucrative outrage industry and an underground white supremacist movement that is causing a great deal of harm in our society.

The "great replacement" conspiracy theory of demographic change, promoted on media outlets from Fox News to 8chan, was taken to heart by the killers who attacked in Charleston, S.C., Christchurch, New Zealand, and, most recently, in El Paso. It also seems to fuel President Trump's efforts, not only to stop illegal immigration, but to remove other people of color from the country. This includes thousands of Nicaraguan refugees who were ordered to leave the country earlier this year, despite living here for decades, as well as the family members of Filipino World War II veterans, who were allowed to stay in the U.S. while waiting for their green cards until about a week ago, when Trump rescinded the permission.

But as hard as these people may try, they're doomed to fail. They can no more stop the tide of demographic change than King Canute could stop the tide of the ocean.

In the process, though, many anxiety sufferers seem to be going out of their way to make things worse. A day hardly passes that we don't see a new video of some idiot telling a person of color to "go back where you came from," or read a story about some lady from Raleigh unrepentantly using the N-word in public. Worse, hate crimes against people of color have risen precipitously every year for about a decade now.

It's almost as if their purveyors want to create as much racial resentment among Black and brown people as they can.

Setting aside for a few moments the insidiousness of racism; its reliance on false, negative stereotypes; its unjust privilege and insistence that "this isn't your land, this is my land"; it's also stupid for practical reasons.

To the "racially anxious": does it make sense to alienate the people who will make up a majority of the population? Does it make sense to lecture them about "assimilation" for only wanting to live their lives with the same kind of comfort and freedom in which you live yours?

A shrewd people, facing inevitable demographic changes,

would reject the harsh voices of resentment that are telling them to be afraid and angry.

A shrewd people would learn how people of color see things, including their experiences with a white majority. Read their books. Watch their movies.

A shrewd people would promote a world-class education system, and one that is highly integrated, so that all of our children would be prepared to take the reins of leadership and work together with knowledge and compassion.

A shrewd people would know which way the wind blows and prepare a soft landing — for everyone.

Sure, there are cultural differences between white, Black and brown people, and they may be uncomfortable. But we also have a shared humanity and a shared desire to be treated with dignity and respect. We all have the ability to find pleasure in learning about others and in creating friendships. There are goals that communities can share regardless of color.

A shrewd people would work for a shared future of peace rather than one of hatred, division and resentment.

Above the planet on a wing

Sep 22, 2019

I've been making friends with the crows.

There's a noisy flock at Quarry Park, and several months ago, I started carrying peanuts with me during my morning walks — two or three times a week — in an attempt to, well, befriend them.

A fanciful desire, absolutely. I didn't really think they'd wind up sitting on my shoulder singing "Whistle While You Work" or anything, but I hoped they'd surrender a little bit of their natural apprehension of people and allow me to observe them from up close, knowing that I was bringing them tasty treats. I hoped they'd come to recognize me, as they've been known to do occasionally with others.

I made a point of arriving at the same time, around sunrise. I'd drop a few peanuts — raw in the shell, no salt — in the same spot, then walk away some distance and wait. I always wore a black t-shirt and black shorts to make myself more recognizable, hoping they might see me as a really big one of them. (She who brightens my days says it's more likely they'd think I'm a really big peanut.)

Early on, one or two hungry crows would fly into nearby trees, calling their presence, and hesitate a minute before swooping down to peck away at the peanuts or grab one and fly away. That quickly became the norm.

One morning when I arrived, a group of six appeared at the top of the trees to the east of the parking lot, barking and cawing as if to say, "Hey, where've you been?" They flew ahead of me to the drop-off spot, waited for me to walk away, then all swooped down for their treats.

I felt like I was hanging out with the cool kids.

I've been interested in crows for some time, actually. They're fascinating, with their rich and complex social and cultural lives. (They mate for life, devote years to raising their young and live in extended family groups. They roost together in large groups at night.)

They've been considered clever since the days of Aesop — an opinion that modern-day experiments confirm. They're featured in our mythology and fables as tricksters and storytellers. Cave dwellers scratched their images on their walls.

In the past, some superstitiously associated them with evil and death. Some people today see them as pests, while the wiser consider them beneficial, since they eat many agricultural pests.

They're pretty, with their dark, glossy coats. Their language is dynamic and emotive. They hop along or even stroll on their slender legs, somehow looking sturdy, clownish and graceful all at the same time.

And they're deft at people.

"Unlike most wild creatures, crows tolerate human habitations and relish the benefits of living within them — mainly the easy food sources," writes Lyanda Lynn Haupt in "Crow Planet." "But to say that crows enjoy human company, or even prefer to live near humans, would be an overstatement."

Indeed, I've recently begun to feel like I've worn out my welcome.

As my visits have increased, the crows have grown blasé to my presence. They don't meet me at the feeding spot anymore. Some mornings they don't show up at all.

I reached out to some local experts — Ron Morris, who writes the Journal's Bird's-Eye View column, and Forsyth County Extension Agent Phyllis Smith. They were both informative, but neither of them could guess at the crows' absence.

One morning I was texting my she: "The crows didn't show up this morning. I think they have a different agenda than me." And that's when it hit me.

Of course they have a different agenda than me. Surely they don't wake up thinking, *is that big peanut here yet?* They have things to do, nests to build, gossip to spread. They might be busy with a sprouting patch of berries or some big fatty worms. I can't read their minds.

And isn't that just the way it is? "The thief thinks everyone would steal," goes the old saying; we expect everyone to think as we do and want what we want — in personal tastes, in politics, in all sorts of things.

But we can no more read people's minds than I can read the crows' wild psyches. Maybe we should give the mind-reading a rest and listen to what people actually say, watch what they actually do.

I'm probably going to give my crow friends a rest for a while. I'll turn my attention to the calm of the morning, with the now-waning moon peeking over my shoulder and the rising sun illuminating patches of trees as the clouds meander by. That's not a bad agenda.

Where the path trails off

Dec 8, 2019

It was time for a driveabout, so I threw some clothes in the car and headed southeast toward the flatlands.

U.S. 421 took me past Siler City, Sanford, Lillington, Dunn and other spots on the map before switching to the two-lane N.C. 242. In a few short hours I was sitting on a pier above the crystal-clear waters of White Lake.

The day was moderately warm for November and I lingered a while before going down the road for lunch at Melvin's Diner in Elizabethtown. Yes, I would drive a hundred and fifty miles for one of Melvin's cheeseburgers. Well, for two.

I spent the night in Whiteville and had breakfast at Penn's Grill, a brightly lit diner with a few eclectic choices, before heading to Lake Waccamaw, where I intended to spend the day hiking its lakeshore trail to the Waccamaw River. After only an hour, though, scattered rain sent me back to my car.

Fortunately, I had a book. I always have a book.

The next morning, early, I headed west toward Fair Bluff, where I thought I'd pause for a few minutes. The sun shined low over my shoulder as I passed former forestland, cleared a century ago to grow cotton.

I'd gone to Fair Bluff the previous year to explore its vaunted tourist attraction, a sturdy boardwalk that follows the Lumber

River through swampland for more than a mile. Unfortunately, Hurricane Florence had demolished significant parts of the boardwalk, so I didn't get far. Florence's floodwaters had also left Fair Bluff's short one-block downtown in ruins.

But the shattered segments had been repaired. I zipped up my jacket and walked the entire length of the raised, leaf-covered boardwalk, listening to distant crows and nearby songbirds. I startled a river otter, which wanted nothing to do with me and dove away.

At the end of the boardwalk, a path continued into the swamp. With the sun still hanging low, I walked through a brown and russet landscape of tall pine, water-logged cypress and ferns. I was overcome by pops of yellow, gold, rust and red leaves and the black water of the river reflecting blue from the sky. The path seemed to end and I sat by the river, at peace with the world.

I hadn't expected this part of the trip to be its highlight.

Eventually it was time to go home, so I took the blue highways through Rowland, Laurinburg, Star. When the radio offered nothing I wanted, I just drove and thought — about big things and nothing.

There can be moments of loneliness during trips like this, but having been single most of my adult life, I've learned how to be alone. It's a skill. It can be rewarding, too, affording the time and freedom to pursue interests that otherwise might be out of reach.

But solitude isn't easy for everyone. A friend who calls herself an introvert tells me that she still needs company. "It's as if I get full of words, and there's a faucet on my back to let them out, but I can't reach it. I need someone else to open it for me."

Some say that our society is in a crisis of loneliness, expressed in growing rates of depression and suicide. It's a crisis that's exacerbated by pressures of all sorts, including angry, divisive politics and a lack of confidence about the future. I feel those pains. Emotional isolation can be excruciating. And it can be worse during the holidays, when some look around and see everyone else surrounded by family and friends and they feel like they're the only ones who are alone.

I've been there.

But I know that it doesn't last; things change.

I look at past situations and wonder — how did I get from there to here?

I can't always retrace the steps; they were incremental. But they added up.

If you're reading this and dreading the season, when everybody but you seems to be happy and connected, I want you to know: Things change. They just do.

Of course, you can take action to speed things along. You can put yourself where people are, even if it's just in a bookstore or a movie theater. You can reach out to the people you know, even if just to briefly say hello. You can volunteer.

Andy Hagler, the executive director of the Mental Health Association of Forsyth County, told me recently, "Volunteering is a great way to focus outside of ourselves and can help people feel more connected, feel like they are contributing, helping others and thus warding off feelings of depression, loneliness, isolation."

So you can call Holly Beck at 336-721-3411 and say, "I'm interested in delivering meals on wheels. How do I get started?" You can call Laurie Coker at the Green Tree Peer Center, 336-577-3743, and say, "What's going on?"

Or you can look up one of these: https://greatnonprofits.org/city/winston-salem/NC

And you can always call the National Suicide Prevention Lifeline: 1-800-273-TALK (8255) and say, "I need help."

You may feel all alone, but you're not. Things change. I promise.

On the brink of the break

Jan 26, 2020

Traffic lights are a revolutionary innovation. They allow millions of people to move freely, more or less, across significant distances while avoiding deadly accidents. So I thought two Fridays ago while sitting at my *third red light in a row.*

A trivial complaint, I know. Privileged, even. My impatience with traffic lights is what we would call a first-world problem, right up there with the dishwasher taking too long or the toast burning unevenly. Tell it to the refugees sitting on the border, wondering if they'll eat today.

All these thoughts passed through my head as I made my way, on this cloudy day, to the Knight Brown Nature Preserve near Stokesdale, a park I'd wanted to visit ever since my colleague, Walt Unks, wrote about it in November. It sounded like a great place to escape the woes of modern-day living for a little while.

Which I needed. I'd been thinking about what New York Times columnist Nicholas Kristof calls "deaths of despair" — deaths attributable to alcohol, drugs and suicide, acerbated by the lack of economic opportunities and/or medical insurance. They seem on the upswing in many parts of both small-town and big-city America, including some of my favorite parts of North Carolina. Kristof cites contributing factors like lack of education, disappearance of well-paying jobs, proliferation of opioids, rising housing costs and increased incarceration.

He's not alone in his conclusions; he echoes many medical and mental-health authorities that warn that the crisis is here and will get worse.

I parked at the preserve and looked over the map posted by the parking lot. I carried my new walking stick, made from a bamboo stalk found in a junk pile in Washington Park. Lightweight, it makes a little whistle when swung.

Not far onto the first leaf-covered trail, deer in the distance ran away, white tails fluttering. Crows cawed to each other.

The stock market is reaching new heights almost daily, but what does that mean for workers, some 50% of whom haven't found the wherewithal to invest? While the market rises, their weekly salaries have increased around 5% or 7%, depending on who's counting. All those new high-end apartment complexes we're seeing — who can afford them? And those who can't, like some of the long-term residents moving out of the Cloverdale Apartments, scheduled to be demolished to make room for more expensive apartments — where will they live?

Deaths of despair occur when the challenges of modern-day living crash through weakened reservoirs of hope; when so much seems to be going wrong that there's no right to be found. And as I walked, I found myself thinking: *Maybe we're not doing this right.*

Maybe there's a better way to provide health care than through insurance companies that demand profits in the billions while rationing care. (On Tuesday, the American College of Physicians officially endorsed single-payer health care.) Maybe there's a better way to run an economy than shoveling all the money to a few at the top of the ladder. (A new study published in the Journal of Epidemiology & Community Health suggests that raising the national minimum wage by $1 an hour could lower the suicide rate significantly — $2 per hour, even more so.) Maybe there's a better way to run our politics than spending obscene amounts of money on elections. Maybe there's a better way to manage traffic.

It's easy to point the finger at politicians, but we all decide what kind of society we'll live in. We decide with how we vote, but also with how we spend our money and how we treat one another. We decide with the expectations we formulate, with what we imagine to be possible, desirable and essential. Sometimes we decide with our indifference.

I'm not suggesting that we abandon capitalism and become good socialists. But maybe our policies need to be tweaked a little to benefit more people. Maybe there's another "ism" that we haven't thought of yet, one that would increase hope and prosperity and diminish despair.

I walked every trail in the preserve, among mossy rocks and rushing streams. There was a lovely, bright green patch of what I'm told is called "Crow's Feet," and a balanced stone cairn constructed by a thoughtful artisan. Time quietly dissolved. And I realized that one thing our society does right, when we do it, is conserve nature. Conservancy allows wildlife and plants to thrive and saves something of this planet from our worst destructive impulses.

There's something refreshingly humble about land conservation. There's something about it that says, "This is already good; let's not ruin it."

I'm told that people feel something similar when adopting pets; they're saving something that could so easily be lost.

I don't know the answers to all of our problems. But I do know that if you want to keep getting what you're getting, you keep doing what you're doing.

If we want something different, we have to do something different.

Color of the sky as far as I can see

Feb 16, 2020

The truth is, I feel cheated.

We generally get one or two snowstorms every winter, heavy enough to coat the ground, stop traffic, empty the bread and milk racks and make everything look like a Christmas card. Just enough to be refreshing, but not debilitating.

Of course, we also get a lot of *wintry mix*.

But this year, we had that pretty flurry about 10 days ago, none of which stuck. That's about it, so far.

I feel cheated.

I anticipate that snowfall every winter. I still remember one of last winter's storms, frosting the ground, the roads, the trees. I put on my wool jacket and knitted cap and marched down the middle of Second Street, the only audible sound the crunch from my boots on the icy crust.

I walked a loop from downtown to Old Salem and back, mostly solitaire, but sometimes waving to others who were outside, spellbound like me. The flakes kept falling, fat and wet, backlit by streetlights.

My breath blossomed in ice crystals. Time stood still.

Later, there was hot chocolate.

Now I fear that the influence of climate change may have stolen one of my most beloved joys.

The lack of snow isn't the only tangible sign of change. Every spring I have to turn the air conditioner on a little earlier than the year before, and keep it on longer. I much prefer open windows. I much prefer North Carolina's four distinct seasons.

Of course, people in other parts of the world are suffering worse consequences. Islands are sinking beneath rising sea water. Hundreds of Europeans die annually in record-breaking summer heat waves. And then there's Australia. Even under the most optimistic projections, we're going to be dealing with climate change for generations.

But I'm allowed to miss my snowfall — aren't I? It's a treasure, practically a birthright, that may have been stolen from all of us.

Of all the issues we face these days, climate change in particular makes me feel helpless. It's not going to be fixed with a few electric cars. It'll only be reversed — or mitigated — through widespread institutional changes that seem unlikely — and that are opposed by powerful, influential forces.

But there may be hope.

On Friday, The Washington Post reported an alliance of corporations (including big oil companies), environmental advocacy groups, economists and prominent citizens that bills itself as "the broadest climate coalition in U.S. history." It offers an ambitious plan that includes a variety of approaches to tackling climate change. More about that in the future.

Even more significant, perhaps, the coalition includes members of the Republican Party, which is finally waking up to the necessity of tackling the problem.

"In poll after poll, large numbers of young and suburban Republican voters are registering their desire for climate action and say the issue is a priority. And their concern about climate change is spreading to older GOP supporters, too," reporter Steven Mufson wrote in a Washington Post story earlier this month. He profiled several Republican leaders who are forging a new approach, including Rep. Bruce Westerman, a graduate of Yale University's forestry school, who has authored a bill calling for the planting of a trillion trees, which would soak up atmospheric carbon dioxide like a sponge.

Well, knock me over with a spoon. This is good news indeed.

But all is not puppies and roses. Later in the story, Mufson quotes Rep. Garret Graves, R-La., saying, "Democrats like sticks and we like carrots. We're not out there dreaming about unicorns. We're talking about taking fact-based solutions."

And I think: Does *everything* have to be partisan?

And I think: *Excuse me? While you and James Inhofe were throwing snowballs at each other on the Senate floor, Democrats were begging you to stop playing with unicorns. They've been doing the heavy lifting on this problem for decades. Don't waltz in here 10 minutes ago and act like you're Joe Climate. Show a little respect.*

The Energy Innovation and Carbon Dividend Act endorsed by the bipartisan Climate Solutions Caucus puts money in taxpayer pockets. How's that for a carrot? The same is true of the carbon-tax plan promoted by Reagan administration veterans George Shultz and James A. Baker.

This new coalition promises *lots* of carrots.

Not having your home flooded or burned out — how's that for a carrot? How about clean air that won't send children with respiratory problems to the hospital every summer? How about an annual snowfall?

Don't get me wrong. Even if our Republican friends are late to the party, they're welcome, as are their suggestions. They could be heroes. Their participation could turn the tide (no pun intended).

And they *could* do so in a fashion that unites Americans rather than pushing them apart. How about giving that a try?

Do they have a snowball's chance? Do we?

I hope, I hope, I hope so.

Tiny paws up the hill

Mar 1, 2020

So I was reading about that legislative candidate in Wilmington who had his female employees wrestle in a tub of grits for a promotion. And —

And, you know what? The hell with him. Let's talk about foxes.

Sleek red-furred foxes live among us, on hills in wooded areas and even under house porches and sheds. While we're snoring, they trot around on dark, soft-padded feet, long, thick tails trailing behind them, pert ears rotating as they prepare to pounce onto mice and voles. They screech at each other as if they were Billy Corgan. Then they sleep away the day the way we might if we could. February is nesting season, during which vixens are likely to hide away in underground dens while giving birth. In a few weeks, we may start catching glimpses of little balls of chocolate fur with bewildered expressions on their faces.

In recent months, I've become obsessed with these graceful, playful beauties. I've read books about their lives, watched hundreds of YouTube videos and sought stories of local encounters. Those I've heard are much like mine.

I've only caught quick glimpses of foxes myself; once, about two years ago while walking in Old Salem and another time last year while walking in Quarry Park. But I think about them often, especially when my mind is ready for a break. I imagine them bouncing quietly by underneath my windows. I imagine getting close enough to offer a treat — which certainly wouldn't be a good long-term habit, but once or twice I think would be OK.

By definition, they're canine, but there seems to be something feline about them as well.

They've been very successful, populating four continents and countless folk tales. They're extremely adaptable, can eat almost anything and can survive a wide range of climes with only their jaws, their paws and the fur on their backs.

When it comes time for a driveabout, I have to take two or three books, all those magazines I've been meaning to read, shorts in case it's warm, a wool jacket in case it's cold, my laptop, my walking stick, seltzer water and snacks. And my phone.

No self-respecting fox would ever allow me to travel with her.

Some few people have started keeping foxes as pets, which I'm not sure is wise. They reportedly can't be housebroken (the foxes) and are so energetic that anything left unsupervised within their reach will quickly become a shredded plaything.

But wild urban foxes are practically model citizens, content to go their own shy way while we boldly go ours. Incidents of interspecies conflict, in terms of rabies, theft or attacks on house pets, are far more imaginary than real. They have more to fear from us.

Earlier this month, I came across a disturbing story about a contest organized by a private hunting club in Maryland to see who could kill the most foxes in one day. The winner of the contest received about $400 after killing 38 foxes, which were piled together before being thrown away — nobody eats foxes, and the high-powered weapons used to kill them leaves the fur unusable.

"Wildlife killing contests are cruel, pointless, and counter to science-based wildlife management," Emily Hovermale, the state's Humane Society director, told a Washington Post reporter. "Marylanders appreciate foxes and other wildlife and want them to be protected from cruelty — not brutally killed for cash, prizes and bragging rights and then thrown away like trash."

Legislation intended to end such practices sits in the Maryland state House.

No county in North Carolina allows such wholesale slaughter of foxes. Forsyth County has a fox season with "a daily bag limit of 2 and season limit of 10. Foxes taken under this season may not be bought or sold," according to the North Carolina Wildlife Resources Commission.

"Most hunters care deeply about conservation and being as humane as possible while maintaining the guidelines set forth by people who study our animal populations and design programs to keep them healthy," Christopher Cox, a military veteran and hunting advocate, told the Post.

I'm certain that most hunters are responsible people. Nevertheless, it doesn't bother me that sport hunting is a hobby in decline. From a peak of about 17 million hunters nationwide in the early 1980s, the number has dropped to about 11.5 million in 2016, according to data from U.S. Fish and Wildlife Service. Our world is constantly changing, and hunters may someday be as rare as toothpick collectors.

The foxes, though, are more likely to endure.

When the space aliens finally arrive, if they demand to be taken to our leader, oh, boy, we'll have a situation on our hands. But interstellar travelers would likely be smart enough to look elsewhere for intelligent life. They may go to the foxes, the crows, the dolphins — the truly evolved beings that have no need for baggage or complicated politics. They may ask, "How do you put up with those frail furless things that cause so much destruction?"

I wonder that sometimes myself.

The last social outing

Mar 29, 2020
(One week into the COVID-19 pandemic lock-down)

It was two Sunday mornings ago that my friends from Greensboro, Tom Henson and Bob Beerman, met me at Quarry Park for a morning hike. We hadn't seen each other in about a month, so we were eager to catch up.

Tom is a retired engineer; Bob sells and repairs high-end double basses. We met through a meditation group and from there followed other mutual interests: hiking, exploring, philosophizing, joking. Tom and I have gone bike-riding together — I can't keep up with him — and I sometimes go to Greensboro to listen to Bob and his wife, Teresa, play music in a wine bar. Over the past three years or so, we've become good friends.

We started walking on the Waughtown Connector on the south side of the quarry, where the woods were still so brown and denuded by winter that we could see deep into them, see the contour of the hills and gullies stretching to the west. Some trees were pale and bare of bark, reminiscent of skeletons. But tiny little violets bloomed all around us. Bob, like me, carried a walking stick; Tom was bare-handed.

We talked and laughed as we walked; not about anything in particular, just the casual sort of conversation you have when you're comfortable with people. We might have mentioned books we'd read or sayings we'd heard or TV shows we'd all seen when we were younger.

We paused at a wooden kiosk with a park map and park rules.

"Where are we?" Bob asked.

Tom pointed to the "you are here" spot, but it took Bob a few breaths to orient himself.

It is a little odd. The entrance to the park is to its north, but somehow, driving up Quarry Road, I always feel like I'm driving north rather than south. The maps in the kiosks are skewed a little, too, with north positioned to the northwest. I mean, northeast.

We returned to the quarry, then walked north, down toward the Peachtree Greenway. The lack of foliage presented views of the lake that are hidden the rest of the year. We paused by the gate near the water's edge and examined the tall granite face on the other side. We paused on the bridge crossing the stream that, as far as I know, has no name.

At one spot, the pavement ended abruptly, but a trail continued into the woods.

"Should we walk on?" one of us asked.

"The rules didn't say, 'no walking off the paved trail,'" one of us said. "They said, 'please stay on paved trail.'"

"Is this even part of the park?" one of us asked.

We walked on into the woods, downward to a rushing stream, where we stood for a while before jumping across. We climbed a hill and saw a lump on the next hill that turned out to be an old Nissan pickup, buried in kudzu.

"How did this get here?" one of us asked. No road is visible now.

A little farther, Bob stopped abruptly and said, "Look — a gray fox."

"Where?" I asked.

Bob pointed: "There."

Tom said, "Yeah. It's pretty."

I kept looking, but I couldn't see it: No reddish fur, as usually grows around a gray fox's neck and belly; no dark eyes; no movement. I strained my eyes — and just couldn't see it.

"It's gone now," Bob said.

"Look," Tom pointed. "There's the trail where it walks every day." The slender foot trail cut away into the distance.

I was disappointed. As I wrote last month, I'm fascinated by the urban red foxes around us. I've only glimpsed a couple as they ran from me, but it seems like everyone I know, friends and neighbors, have had longer sightings. Sometimes their foxes stare back.

We walked on, through the woods, talking and laughing, winding back around to the Waughtown Connector, back to the parking lot, where we said goodbye.

I drove home, and I think that's when it hit me: I didn't know when I'd see my friends again — these or any others.

Then came the stay-at-home order.

I'm usually comfortable with solitude — I don't need any time fillers, I have too many — but it's different when it's not a choice, but an uninvited imposition.

My friends and I are staying in touch via social media. Most Journal staffers are now working from home. The city is quiet. My neighborhood is quiet.

March has been a blur. It's been a month made of mud; cloudy and mostly cold.

I've gone back to Quarry Park by myself several times since that Sunday. I walk to where my friends saw the gray fox. I linger there, kneeling, with the violets at my feet, looking deep into the woods.

In spite of ourselves

Apr 12, 2020

The sky cleared for a couple of days last week, leading me to sit outside early in the morning in the Hernon/Wills Supercollider Observatory (my back porch). The twisty constellation Scorpius hovered in the south; Jupiter rose in the southeast just past the trees to my east, followed by Saturn and Mars. There were shooting stars. There was coffee.

These were calm mornings, and I continued them with walks in Quarry Park, where wisteria perfumed the air and covered *everything*. I'm still looking for the gray fox my friends spotted last month, but all I've seen so far are the dancing white flags of retreating deer tails and crows hungry for the peanuts I carry.

Then it was back to the world.

Even though coronavirus has not affected anyone close to me, I feel the weight of it and mourn for those who have been robbed by it.

I also feel the stress of uncertainty. These last couple of weeks, I've been more short-tempered than usual. I bristle while winding my way through the obstacle course of the grocery store or while being held hostage at red traffic lights with no other traffic in sight. More than once, I counted to 20, as if I were washing my hands. I placed a take-out order with a local restaurant, proud of myself for supporting the local economy, and was chagrined by the abruptness of the man on the other end of the phone. But when I arrived to pick up my food, I saw that he was very gracious. It was a misunderstanding of tone, as often occurs with email or other forms of communication that don't include facial expression.

I imagine others have had similar experiences.

Of course, many of us are looking for meaning in the current crisis, some lesson we can take from it — as if that would justify its tragedy. Some want to blame it on the usual suspects — whatever they were already against: Porous borders, other people, the other political party, the mysterious "them." Some blame President Trump, who blames everyone else.

I'm just like anyone else. My usual suspects — not to cause the biological virus, but to exacerbate its effects — include the failure of the United States, singular among all the world's advanced nations, to provide adequate health insurance for its own people. Here we are, in the 21st century (people used to say, "Here we are, in the 18th century") still linking income and insurance to work when we know that arrangement fails.

Some of us are thinking to the days ahead and hoping we can get back to normal. Others say we'll have a new normal — no more handshaking, for one thing — and they welcome it, hoping this crucial event can be a springboard to fix some of the societal problems that have existed for far too long.

I don't know if Twitter helps or hurts more in a time like this, but it did expose me last week to this nugget of wisdom:

> *Ethics Gradient*
> *@grahamvsworld*
> *My 5yo stormed out of my office when i told him i had to do a meeting. He was very mad that i couldn't look at his crafts like i did yesterday. I tried to explain that it was Monday and I had to work, and he yelled "Monday isn't real!" on the way out. I'm still just sitting here.*

If we learn nothing else, I think "Monday isn't real" is plenty.

I'm starting to think that money isn't real, either, especially when government can find as much of it as it wants for anything it wants. I'm telling you, that Universal Basic Income is starting to look better — and more possible — all the time.

I'm keeping my own list of things that I wish could change when we finally emerge from our cocoons. Among them:

That we stop glorifying busy-ness and pushing ourselves so hard that we get sick.

That we stop uncritically associating wealth with virtue.

That we all learn to be a little more grateful and a little more patient. Yep, me too.

Since I'm wishing, I'll add eight-day weeks with three-day weekends; no cars allowed downtown, only bicycles and golf carts — and delivery trucks in back alleys; and the steady elimination of light pollution — and every other kind of environmental pollution.

The coronavirus is a historic event, the casualties of which have already long surpassed the 9/11 attack. And while it's unlikely that we could have completely avoided it, it's beyond dispute that we could have been better prepared. Point the finger where you will, observers in positions of authority saw it coming and tried to warn us, but were ignored. The wealthiest nation in history didn't have the proper medical equipment for workers on the front line, and some of them have died because of that failing.

If we don't learn a lesson from that, we are surely among the biggest fools in history, too.

We all will be received

Apr 25, 2020

When this craziness is all over, I'm going to take U.S. 158 across the top of the state to Elizabeth City on the Inner Banks. I'll check into a rustic B&B and walk through the aged downtown, poking my nose into consignment shops, looking at knickknacks and novelties.

In the morning, I'll order a waffle at Andy's Pancake and Steak House, then go to Waterfront Park and watch the wind whip the waves on the Pasquotank River.

That may take a few hours.

When I'm tired of sitting, I'll go to the lengthy boardwalk behind the College of the Albemarle and stroll around for a little while. Then I'll go to the Recycled Reader and buy a new stack of books to set on the floor.

Later I'll drive north to the Great Dismal Swamp and ride my bike down the bumpy Washington Ditch trail to Lake Drummond, thinking about the wildlife, reluctant to be seen, in the woods around me. I'll wonder if there are foxes.

When this is all over, my friends Tom and Bob and I are going to go camping at Goose Creek State Park by the Pamlico River. We'll build a campfire and roast marshmallows, laughing at fart jokes late into the night like a bunch of 12-year-olds. The next morning we'll put kayaks into the river and paddle until we're exhausted and sunburned. Later we'll get dinner in Little Washington and assess all the boats along the waterfront docks, dreaming about life as a mariner.

When this is all over, I'm going to get breakfast at the Lighthouse. Trish will hug me and ask, "How's your dad?"

"Oh, he's fine," I'll answer.

I'll drink too much coffee.

When this is over, I'm going to eat in restaurants. I'm going to go see movies in movie theaters. I'm going to go to Cooks Flea Market and look at all the stuff and buy a hot dog. I'm going to go to the Cobblestone Farmers Market and buy tomatoes. I'm going to go to the Rockford General Store and buy candy. I'm going to hear local bands play and dance in front of the stage. I'm going to hear the Winston-Salem Symphony.

But not . . . dance in front of that stage.

When this is over, I'm going to meet my new grand-nephew, Logan.

When this is behind us, I'm going to walk through all the galleries in the Arts District to remind myself why we have that slogan, anyway. I'll look for a painting that captures the mood of jubilation.

When this is over, I'm going to identify every county in North Carolina in which I've not yet set foot and I'm going to go there.

When this is over, I'm going to take my bike to the Catawba River Greenway in Morganton and the Roanoke Canal Trail in Roanoke Rapids and the Riverwalk Trail in Danville, Va., and the Virginia Creeper. I'm going to finally ride the entire 57.7 miles of the New River Trail from Pulaski to Fries.

When this is over, I'm going to run a marathon.

Well. A half-marathon.

When this is all over, I'm going to go days without checking Twitter. I'm going to read deeply, for hours, with no distractions, and listen to music and spend more time under the stars and less in front of screens.

When this is all over, I'm going to talk to my neighbors. I'll greet all the people I've not been able to see with an affectionate bow.

When this is over, I'll still seek solitude as I need it. I'll still seek company as I desire it. But I'm never going to get upset about a baby crying in a restaurant ever again.

When this is over, I'm going to book a trip to a wildlife sanctuary outside San Diego, where three Russian-bred domestic foxes live: Victor, a dog with a red coat, Mikhail, a dog with a black coat, and Maksa, a vixen with a white coat. I'll hold one in my lap and feed it treats and scratch it behind the ears until it's sick of me.

When this is over, I'm going to take a boat to Sark Island, off the coast of France. I'll bike across the spine of the island, lie down in a field and stay awake all night, watching the stars wheel over my head. Then I'll sleep all day in a tent and wait for the dark to return.

When this is all over, when we can travel freely and walk about without the risk of infecting each other, I'm going to visit desert, mountain, sea and prairie. My motto will be: Don't wait.

When this is over, I'm going to *go*. I'm going to go, go go. And I may not come back.

Who's with me?

The course of a lifetime runs

May 10, 2020

Five newborn fox kits recently appeared in a den above a creek in a nearby suburban park. The location was uncharacteristically close to human traffic and allowed crowds of passersby to take close-up photos and videos of the kits, fuzzy and wide-eyed, greeting the world.

When my friends told me, I was enchanted. That's my jam, you know.

I happened to have some time on my hands and began to spend a few morning and evening hours near the several entrances to their den, hoping to see them myself. While waiting, I spoke with neighbors — all from a proper distance, of course — who told me stories and showed me phone videos of the kits playing while watched over by their mom — strong, but clearly emaciated from non-stop feeding. That's what happens with foxes.

It was never clear to me whether there was a mom and dad or just a mom — both situations exist in the wild — but one morning before sunrise I finally saw the dark silhouette of what I took to be the mom, sliding gracefully down a grassy slope, supremely silence.

The next day I saw what I took to be the dad, strutting down the sidewalk with a squirrel in his mouth. His lush red fur seemed almost neon in the sunlight.

I never saw the kits, and from what I hear, they weren't seen last week, either. It's a bit early for them to move on in search of their own territory; maybe the whole family got tired of being rock stars and retreated to a new home.

Fox mothers have a good reputation. They're both playful and patient as they raise and teach their kits. And they're very protective, sometimes going head to head with hungry coyotes and badgers, even though those beasts are more ferocious.

They're less assertive with people. I've followed a couple of stories in which wildlife control professionals were called in to move the inhabitants of a newly developed den from underneath a porch or a shed. In both instances, they took the kits, one by one, very gently, and placed them in a safe, accessible container before closing off the den. In the meantime, the mothers paced in the distance.

But after the pros left, the mothers returned and carried the kits, one by one, by the scruff of the neck to new homes.

I don't blame the moms for being apprehensive; they're only human.

Foxes have been known to bury their dead kits. One story I followed told of a pair of foxes that did so, and would return from time to time to the burial site. We can't read foxes' minds, but I can't help imagining that they visited out of sorrow, as we might do.

I have a dear friend who is a mother of three. She had to go back to work last week.

Her job, which is considered essential (by her employer), requires her to spend hours in several different grocery stores, handling merchandise in the midst of shoppers. She chose to take a leave of absence during the shutdown order, but felt pressured to return to work to ensure her job security.

Two of my friend's children have immune systems that are compromised. Her daughter has Down syndrome and a heart defect. To most, she doesn't seem very communicative, but her mother can read her mind. She interprets her discomfort and desires from small, non-verbal cues.

My friend must now take the risk of being around other people, then returning home, possibly carrying something deadly with her. She goes through a daily come-home protocol that involves thorough bathing, scrubbing everything with Lysol and wearing mask and gloves when with her daughter.

"If it were a matter of another month or two," she told me, "I might try to hold out longer. But we're going to be living with this for a year or two and I can't afford to quit. So I've got to adapt. I have to treat it as another unavoidable risk in life."

"The worst part of it," she told me, "is the anxiety that hangs over me before I even wake up. The fear that I could bring home something that could take her from me is heavy on me through the day and in my dreams. That and being afraid of cuddling and comforting her."

My friend and I have discussed options and there don't seem to be any outside of winning the lottery. All she can do is take the risk and worry.

She's not the only one, of course.

So when I hear about these goobers who are *so certain* that the virus isn't dangerous that they're willing to bet other peoples' lives, I get a little upset.

"We can't let them normalize the fear," they say, hips swaying under the weight of their holsters.

All I can do is ask you to do what I'm doing: Please, please, wear a mask. Wash your hands. Lobby your legislators to improve workers' rights. Encourage others to do so. And join me, next year, in celebrating another Mother's Day.

When the levee breaks

Jun 7, 2020

I saw it coming.

It was Tuesday afternoon and the TV in the office was full of images of thousands and thousands of young protesters, spread across the country — D.C., Los Angeles, New York and smaller cities — while the crawl at the bottom of the screen told us that curfews were coming at 6 p.m., 7 p.m., 8 p.m., depending on the place.

I knew the protesters weren't going to leave — there was too much energy in the air — and I feared for what would happen then. Federal troops had been deployed and President Trump was urging governors to break down hard on demonstrators.

I'm not a fortune teller. But I learned this lesson years ago: *Where you draw the line, that's where the fight will be.*

President Trump had a hand in drawing the line. In fact, he was its architect. He'd been working to change the narrative from a fight over the unjust killing of George Floyd and countless other Black and brown men and women into a fight over "law and order." Over "domination."

"Today, I have strongly recommended to every governor to deploy the National Guard in sufficient numbers that we dominate the streets," he said during a televised address from the Rose Garden on Monday. "Mayors and governors must establish an overwhelming presence until the violence is quelled." Then, just after he declared himself "an ally of all peaceful protesters," the peaceful protesters lingering in Lafayette Square were teargassed and rubber-bulleted to clear the way from the White House to St. John's Episcopal Church. People were hurt. Badly.

Trump, surrounded by a suited entourage and phalanx of troops, marched across the street, dominating it. He stood in front of the church, fidgeting a Bible in his hands, then he held it up in the air like a trophy. Dominating it.

St. John's rector, the Rev. Gini Berbasi, had been at the church, assisting protesters, when federal police moved in and removed her. It was Jesus' cleansing of the Temple, but in reverse; chasing out the devout so the money lenders could take possession.

Later, the Rev. Mariann Edgar Budde, the Episcopal bishop of Washington, D.C., said she was outraged by Trump's actions, calling it an "abuse of sacred symbols" and "antithetical to the teachings of Jesus and everything that our churches stand for." Among the other insults, Trump didn't have the decency to ask permission to stage a photo op.

But dominators don't ask. They take.

Nebraska Sen. Ben Sasse was among the few Republicans who objected later: "There is no right to riot, no right to destroy others' property, and no right to throw rocks at police," he said in a statement. "But there is a fundamental — a Constitutional — right to protest, and I'm against clearing out a peaceful protest for a photo-op that treats the Word of God as a political prop."

But he should have saved himself the trouble. Trump has already dominated the Republican Party. He's dominated dozens of news cycles. He dominated his own impeachment. What won't he try to dominate?

Tuesday evening, after the curfews passed, I waited for the breaking news. Across the country, surely the report would come: Chaos. Bloodshed. Domination.

But it didn't. By Wednesday morning, it was clear that all across the nation, cooler heads prevailed. Marchers marched, sang, waved signs, shut down traffic — and the authorities moved the line to accommodate them.

That's not to say there weren't exceptions. Particularly later in the week, reports came in from across the nation of violent incidents — many instigated by police officers. In New York City in particular, it seemed as if the police officers were rioting.

But for the most part, the peace held.

This, despite Trump's best efforts, tweeting Tuesday night for New York to call up the National Guard, referring to protesters as "lowlifes and losers," reminiscent of the way he once defined illegal immigrants as "criminals" and "rapists" — except this time, he was talking about his own country's citizens.

By Wednesday morning, Defense Secretary Mark Esper, who had marched to St. John's with Trump, was trying to distance himself from the incident and affirmed that he wouldn't allow military forces to quell protests. Attorney General William Barr took the bullet — sorry, bad turn of phrase — claiming that he'd ordered the clearing, not Trump. There was "no correlation," he said, between the clearing and Trump's walk to the church. Sure, just a coincidence.

On Wednesday, former Defense Secretary James Mattis finally spoke out against what he called Trump's "bizarre photo op," which he called "an abuse of executive authority." On Thursday, the ACLU and Black Lives Matter filed suit against the Trump administration for its violent clearing of Lafayette Square. This isn't over by a long shot.

Even as Trump evokes the memory of George Floyd, it doesn't seem like he understands what this is all about. He's still trying to redefine the battle line, demanding that Americans choose between the Prince of Peace or the King of Domination; between taking a knee or kneeling on a neck.

I put this column to bed on Friday, two days before you're reading it, and I don't know what the weekend holds. But I feel optimistic.

Trump won't dominate the streets. They belong to the American people.

A lucky man who made the grade

Jun 21, 2020

Last Saturday morning, I sat in front of the TV and turned it to Fox News.

Six hours later, I turned it off, disgusted. In all that time, there hadn't been a single story about foxes.

Maybe I misunderstood something.

I'm not alone, though; I sometimes receive feedback from readers that, while welcome, reveals misunderstandings about the nuts and bolts of our operation here on Marshall Street.

To some degree, I think, it's our own fault; we don't always do a great job of explaining ourselves.

But for fun and edification, let me drop a couple of examples while making it clear that for the purposes of this column, I'm not talking about my section of the paper, where we endlessly opine, but just the straight-ahead news department, where reporters, photographers and news editors work.

A few weeks ago, a reader told me that our recent stories about Sen. Richard Burr's stock trades "did nothing to convince me that he's done anything illegal." To which I say: good. News stories aren't supposed to persuade; they're supposed to tell you what happened. They might also provide context, including historical data or the reactions of influential people, but their purpose is to inform, not advocate.

More recently, a reader suggested to me that the Black Lives Matter protests in Winston-Salem might stop if we stopped reporting them. This reminded me of the liberal complaints following the 2016 election that all the media coverage of Donald Trump contributed to his election.

But even assuming that halting the protests would be a worthy goal, the job is still to report, not influence. Some people — protesters and presidents — may be savvy enough to take advantage of the press. But like Batman facing a trap he knows was set by the Joker, news professionals still have to step in and report what's happening.

One reader recently told me that the entire Associated Press, a network of thousands of reporters and news outlets, had a liberal bias. But as I read news stories that adhere to the facts, I can't help wondering if the real complaint isn't that the AP doesn't have a conservative bias.

When even President Trump's conservative Supreme Court rules in favor of LGBTQ rights and corporations release statements in support of Black Lives Matter, I have to think that maybe the media isn't so much liberal as reflective of mainstream American values.

"These days, it has become commonplace to make scapegoats of 'the media.' We blame the media for everything: our divided country, our failed policies, our anxieties," Len Niehoff, a University of Michigan Law School professor, wrote recently in The Detroit News. "It has become a national pastime and a drumbeat of political rhetoric. And it's dumb and dangerous."

He continues:

"Many factors have contributed to these developments, including inflammatory statements made by political leaders. But our everyday language about 'the media' has also stoked the fire. Statements that the media are biased, unreliable or dishonest have become ordinary fare in homes, workplaces and social settings. We say them as if they were self-evidently true.

"On close analysis, however, it turns out that these statements are not just wrong, they are gibberish. They treat 'the media' as some sort of monolithic thing, when they are neither monolithic nor a thing. To the contrary, they are so diverse as to make it impossible to generalize about them. And they are made up of human beings."

Being human, reporters don't get it right all the time, of course. Just last week, the aforementioned Fox News got in trouble for doctoring photos on its website to make the Capitol Hill Autonomous Zone in Seattle look more dangerous than it really is. And the New York Times was widely criticized for waffling a headline after Vice President Mike Pence urged governors to lie about COVID-19.

But most reporters, carrying their notepads and cameras, are just trying to do good work, keeping the public informed and spelling the names correctly. They do so while facing difficulties that these days include physical attacks from both protesters and police. They've got my respect.

But while we have world-class reporting at our fingertips, too many of us turn instead to dubious voices for our "news," like phony baloney on social media or the outrage merchants on cable TV. Fifty-six percent of people said they were concerned about what was real and what was fake online and 40% said they were concerned about misinformation on social media, according to a recent Reuters report — and well they should be concerned, especially with coronavirus conspiracies floating around out there in the air like germs.

We need conscientious, reliable news professionals to avoid the bluster and give us the facts, even if we don't like the reports. We need them to tell us what our government is doing. We need them to tell us what's happening on our streets and around the world. Where would we be without them? Uninformed and misinformed.

But enough about the news for today. I want to check out this thing I heard about called The History Channel. Wish me luck.

Weekenders on our own

Jul 5, 2020

It was the perfect sequestered day.

The sun was still low as I approached Horizons Park, taking a little looping detour because of the closure of Memorial Industrial School Road. A group of horses grazed behind a fence, flicking their tails and nuzzling each other. A mob of crows hopped around on the road like little clowns.

The air was cool as I began walking on the park's dirt trail, carrying my trusty bamboo walking stick. The forest, still in shadow, looked mysterious. Birds sang for their breakfast and water trickled through streams bordered by moss and stone. Peaceful.

Back home a couple hours later, I baked eggs for breakfast and had more coffee as I read the news, because I have to. But I soon turned to my book, Sarah Scoles' "They Are Already Here," an entertaining and informative history of America's UFO subculture, and let the world drift away.

Later, I took a quick walk to the neighborhood park, just to stretch my legs. As much as I like to read, too much of it gives me the yawns.

I made lunch and decided on an afternoon matinee of Ridley Scott's lush 2005 film, "Kingdom of Heaven," the superior director's cut. This time, I pretty much understood what was happening, from the Jerusalem court intrigue to its lucid moral: What man is a man who does not make the world better?

The rest of the day and evening was spent in similar solitary pursuits, with occasional breaks to exchange an email or two with distant friends. Eventually I put on the soundtrack to "Hamilton," listening with half an ear while lazily performing a few necessary home chores. And as the ensemble sang about "working through the unimaginable," I stopped and sobbed.

It's a touching song, anyway. But I'd been on the edge of this particular fit for a few days — not the result of any particular event, but an accumulation of subtle pressures, from the personal to the political, heightened by the demands of the worsening coronavirus.

I'm taking sequestration seriously because with our numbers going the wrong way, I'm not, as columnist Leonard Pitts puts it, going to die of stupid. But even for someone like me who is comfortable with solitude, I'm learning the borders of that comfort. I miss being around people. I miss my friends. I fear losing the ability to carry on a conversation for 10 minutes. And I hate to absorb all the bad news of the day on my own.

As I write this, I realize that I'm living a charmed existence. Some people right now are struggling with respirators; some are mourning lost loved ones; some are fighting just to keep a roof over their heads. And some in our community were living with the steady drip of accumulated pressures, sometimes not so subtle, even before the virus hit us.

But still, I weep.

By now we've all heard of and seen the videos of the "Karens," as they're pejoratively called, privileged white women who throw temper tantrums because they're asked to wear masks or because the chef is out of cheese or because a dark-skinned stranger is walking through their neighborhoods. Not everyone under pressure resorts to cheap racial slurs; I doubt any of those spontaneous eruptions are generated by their speakers' first racist thought. It's difficult to muster much sympathy for them.

But in my better moments, I've been reminded that suffering is suffering. And though some handle it better than others — some acquire the tools they need to persevere — there's really no hierarchy. Despite our urge, sometimes, to say, "That's nothing, you should see what I — " it's not a contest. It's not like only the most tormented or tortured people are worthy of being heard and comforted.

You take the daily pressures, then you add the long wait in line; the desperate search for scarce goods; the closed amenities — as trivial as they seem, they may just represent the last straw of a stack that's been piling and piling and piling with no relief in sight.

Sometimes I think it's surprising that we're not all blowing up.

There's a passage from Marcus Aurelius' "Meditations" that's stuck with me over the years. It's too long to print here, but I would paraphrase it like this:

Every day you leave your home and go out into the world. And sometimes you're going to meet jerks; selfish, mean, ignorant jerks. It's unavoidable.

Just remember that you've been a jerk once or twice, too. Jerkiness is just one part of our shared humanity.

We could all use a little grace in this pressured time. If we offer it, maybe we'll receive it as well.

In the meantime, I recommend a good cry.

With autumn closing in

Aug 2, 2020

I woke last night to the sound of thunder.

Actually, it was two Fridays ago, in the wee hours. After a couple of minutes, I realized that the waves going through my brain were the kind that indicate alertness; there would be no going back to sleep. It happens sometimes.

So I got up and put on the coffee, then sat in the Hernon/Wills Supercollider Observatory (my back porch) and watched the storm.

Did you see it? It was dramatic. Through the darkness, lightning shot across the sky as if from Dr. Frankenstein's electrodes. The thunder boomed deeply in the distance like Leonard Cohen's voice. Eventually, rain began to tap on the metal roof over my head and as my feet got wet, thoughts flitted through my head, as they do.

For a while I thought about that old Bob Seger tune, "Night Moves," and there's a lot I could say about it. When it was released in 1977, rock music was important to me not just as entertainment, but culturally. My friends and I discussed song lyrics as if we were translating the Voynich manuscript. Working on mysteries without any clues.

I didn't realize this then, but the song was bold for its day. Presumably aimed at younger listeners, it told the story of an older man reminiscing about his first . . . well, not his first love. His first lover.

But back then, even though I probably didn't understand the message, not as I do now — or catch the nuance of the line, "with autumn closing in" — the music, with its lone acoustic guitar and quiet pauses, conveyed a sense of poignancy. Even at a tender age — I was a high-school senior — it made me feel lonesome.

Seger was in his early 30s at the time. Now in his mid-70s, he might laugh at his temerity then, writing about the autumn of his life. But the song holds up.

On the porch, I pondered other things: weekend plans, a new mission to Mars that launched Thursday. And, inevitably, I tried to make sense of some political thing or other.

Sometimes it feels like there are two realities in American life. There's what happens to us as we walk the streets, going into stores or sitting at our desks at work; walking through the neighborhood looking for foxes. Most exchanges are polite or friendly. (I've been practicing smiling through my mask, hoping people will be able to tell and feel a little cheered, the way other people often cheer me.)

Then there's what the legislators are up to, which we generally learn through the news. Note the study mentioned in today's editorial; we've all known for some time now that Congress can't seem to get anything done. It's too politicized, both sides, and much of the rhetoric we hear is overheated, inaccurate and ridiculous. (Next on my reading list: "The Death of Expertise" by Tom Nichols.)

It's a truism now to note that coronavirus has revealed the weaknesses in our systems of governance and health care, and possibly voting. Not that we can be prepared for every contingency; we can't — but we surely could have been better prepared for this one.

We've got to find a way out. Something's got to give.

Sitting on a porch with a cup of coffee watching a storm, that other reality can seem like a dream. But we can't ignore it. Decisions made in Raleigh and Washington wind up having a tangible effect on us here in Winston-Salem. To be good citizens, we have to pay attention — we have to listen and *think*.

I guess we need a balance.

Eventually the sky brightened and it was time to eat breakfast, read the news and feed the squirrels.

But I enjoyed the storm. I've enjoyed every bit of rain this month, even though it interferes with stargazing. The rain is nice just because it's different.

This is my least favorite season, with such oppressive heat and humidity that it can generate the sort of seasonal affective disorder that some people feel in the winter. Everything feels heavy.

Hurry, autumn.

The circumstances of the virus continue to be challenging, along with the political discord, the sheer uncertainty about how my life and the lives of my friends will go. It's more challenging for people who are struggling to pay rent and keep the kids fed.

But I still feel optimistic. I'm a child of Star Trek, a believer in a brighter future, certain that we can create something wonderful if we just . . . do something different.

How far off? I sit and wonder.

Far away from the bustle

Aug 30, 2020

We made it.

Two more quick flips of the calendar and we're out of this gruesome hot month and on our way into the fall, at least on paper. Orion has returned to the morning sky, with Venus on one side and Mars on the other. A change is gonna come; a change in temperature, light and scenery. I'm ready. I imagine you are, too.

I realized the other day that I've not worn long pants in almost six months.

I attended the streatery last week and recommend it highly; alfresco dining is very refreshing. What a luxury it is to just sit in a restaurant and have a server bring food. I sure took that for granted before.

I also finally attended one of our drive-in theaters, where I managed to stay awake for most of a show. It was a lot of fun to see other people in their cars, laughing and enjoying themselves.

I continue to imitate my wise friends who dull the pain of the current crisis by taking their small pleasures where they can: Comfort food. Music. Books.

And, of course, foxes.

I don't know how I came to be so fascinated by these

beautiful and graceful creatures, but I've been studying them — by which I mean absorbing books, documentaries and videos on YouTube — for months now. I wouldn't call myself an expert, but I'm a smartypants.

Even though it's rare for a fox to have an affectionate bond with a human being — they're wild animals, after all — they do have some interesting interactions with people and with other animals.

I've been following a wildlife aid group in London that rescues urban foxes that have tangled themselves in nets or been injured in some way. They're always wary and rarely show gratitude, but their rescuers are rewarded by helping. Surely the job of fox rescuer is the best job in the world.

I watched a series of videos featuring two fox kits who were abandoned on the doorstep of a Russian veterinarian, who then had little choice but to raise them. I love listening to the vet talk to the kits. I imagine they understand her about as well as I do.

What would it be to be a fox to whom human beings rumble and sing? What do they think we are?

With generous snouts being the norm, do they look at us and think the fox equivalent of, *where's your dang nose?*

One of my favorite things about foxes is that they're such brazen thieves. I watched a video of a man who invited a curious fox into his kitchen. The fox grabbed a shoe lying nearby and ran.

That tickles me to no end. It's not like he was going to wear the shoe, but there it was, so . . .

A great many people have learned that it doesn't hurt to feed foxes sometimes. They don't forget how to hunt and they don't lose their natural apprehension of us. And they don't attack. They're more likely to arrive early and sit, very politely, waiting.

About a month ago, some kind acquaintances had me over to their home, not far from Washington Park, to help them feed a skulk of foxes, as the term goes, that show up daily for dinner.

We sat in the backyard, safely distanced from one another, as five or so foxes appeared over a ridge. My hosts knew each of them; their grandchildren have given them names like Rose, Red and Swiper. They were small, with short summer fur. They dashed about like little red lightning bolts.

Each of us would take a slice of bread, wrap little chunks

of hot dogs inside it, ball it up and toss it out. One of the foxes would grab it and chew it up, open-mouthed.

Swiper seemed the most shy, but he lived up to his name, rushing out to grab a bread ball, then running off with it.

Red was the boldest; she would come right up close to our feet to take a snack. At first she happily chewed the bread balls, but eventually she started filling her mouth with as many of them as she could, then carried them away to store for later, as foxes do. Then she'd come back for more.

At one point Red sat just a few feet away from me. She looked me in the eye and I felt like she recognized me.

It was the highlight of my summer.

There's suffering in the fox world. Sometimes they fight. They get diseases and parasites. In urban settings, they're often run over by cars. There are no doctors or physical therapists in their society; they just keep going as long as they can.

But the fox world is innocent of complication. They don't need clothes or credit cards or insurance forms. They hunt and eat and play and raise kits. They just fox.

I delight in this world we can never control and, with hope, never destroy.

There are many here among us

Sep 20, 2020

Isn't it funny, the things that can rattle around in our heads? I can't tell you what I had for dinner yesterday, but a scene from "The Waltons," the classic family drama set in the Depression era, has been bouncing around up there for months now. I finally looked it up online (fifth season, 1977) and was surprised that I remembered it almost exactly as it happened.

In the episode, John-Boy Walton causes a stir by running portions of "Mein Kampf" in his newspaper, The Blue Ridge Chronicle.

I'm not making this up, honest.

One thing leads to another, culminating in the Rev. Matthew Fordwick (played by John Ritter, no less) organizing a burning of German books — which John-Boy jumps up to stop.

"This is my fault," he says. "I started this whole thing with my newspaper, I know that. But you misunderstood me. I was trying to show you what people are capable of out of ignorance and out of fear and out of hatred. . . .

"I read that a foreign tyrant was publishing his plans to take over the world and was carrying out those plans and I thought you ought to have the opportunity to know about it. Just like I'd take the opportunity to tell you if there was a blight that was threatening your crops or some kind of scandal that was threatening your government, because that's freedom, as far as I can see it.

"And if you choose not to know about it, that's freedom, too, but if you take a book and if you burn this book, then you can't know about it and you've had your freedom taken away from you, you understand me?"

And then he finds, among the kindling, a book that begins, *Am Anfang schuf Gott Himmel und Erde.*

In English: "In the beginning, God created the heavens and the Earth."

The fire is put out, apologies are offered, and peace reigns on Walton's Mountain.

I think about that episode every time someone asks me why we run so many anti-Trump letters in the Journal.

Now, I promise I'm not making a Nazi analogy. And the people who ask me about this — near as I can tell, they're all good folks. They're very civil when they call or write.

But they get tired of reading so many critical letters about the man for whom they voted and support today.

I sympathize. We *do* run a lot of letters that criticize President Trump — more than Barack Obama or George W. Bush before him.

So why do we print them? The easy answer is because we receive them. If a letter is under 250 words, if it's about a topic that's in the news, if it's not too nasty and if its facts check out, we'll likely print it. Them's the rules.

We also receive and print letters that support Trump, we just don't receive very many — though they're picking up ahead of the election. And while I've offered invitations — and still do, *hint, hint* — some readers have declined; they don't want to write letters, they've told me, they just don't want to read so many that they find disagreeable.

Fair enough. But we still receive the letters, so I've asked readers to provide me with an objective criterion — a fair rule that would apply to every letter writer — that would lead to printing fewer anti-Trump letters.

No one has suggested one.

There are, by the way, some letters that oppose Trump that we *don't* print — letters with no substance that just call the president names or insult his physical attributes. The standards of The Readers' Forum are higher than the standards of the president's Twitter feed.

Some readers also tell me that they think we — the media in general — have been unfair to the president. We nit-pick every little thing he does. We didn't scrutinize other presidents this way.

I can't speak for every media outlet. But to me, comparing Trump to other presidents is like comparing apples to platypus. Trump ran for office as a disrupter, and that's one promise he's kept, undermining the missions of bedrock agencies like the EPA, the CDC and the U.S. Census, rolling back important pollution protections and doing, saying or tweeting something outrageous practically *every day*. Plus, you know, he lies an awful lot. Responsible news organizations have to report these things. Not to do so would be an abrogation of responsibility.

But back to John-Boy — why do I think about that TV episode from decades ago?

Because the letter writers — among them, ministers, teachers, business people, health professionals and your neighbors — along with former Trump associates and quite a few Republican officials who now endorse Joe Biden, they're all doing the same thing that John-Boy did:

They're trying to warn you.

But a moment's sunlight

Sep 27, 2020

The last road trip I took, last March before the pandemic altered our lives, was to Rutherfordton, a smallish community of about 4,000 west of Charlotte.

I went because I'd never been there.

On a crisp, cool morning, I warmed up with coffee and breakfast in Greene's Café. While sitting there, I read the local paper, The Daily Courier, and was particularly impressed by the insight of local chicken farmer and columnist Larry McDermott. I still read him online.

After breakfast, I found a farmer's market spilling from the Main Street Deli in the center of downtown onto the sidewalk, with lots of fruits and homemade preserves and bread.

"Is that real sourwood honey?" I asked one vendor.

"We're blessed with many sourwood trees on my property," he answered.

My honey expert later confirmed its quality.

At Next Door Used Books in nearby Forest City, with sunlight warming the store's dark wooden floors, I bought a bundle of books by Manly Wade Wellman, an obscure North Carolina author and contemporary of H.P. Lovecraft. They're hard to find.

There were consignment stores and an arcade museum and The Pie Safe (look it up) and a fountain in the center of town.

It was a delightful trip. And it was the last time I walked freely among other people without wearing a mask.

I miss exploring small North Carolina towns like this and Warrenton, Edenton and Whiteville. The food is always good. The architecture is lovely. I usually wind up having conversations with people who are invariably welcoming and warm.

As much as I love Winston-Salem, I can imagine retiring to a small town, where I wouldn't have to wrestle with traffic lights and could sit under a truly dark, star-filled sky. Someplace where I could feed foxes and crows and the neighbors would offer me fresh eggs and ghost stories.

It would be a lot easier to realize that dream if we weren't losing rural medical facilities by the dozen.

And it would feel a lot more possible if we weren't in the midst of a deadly virus that has killed over 200,000 Americans, a chaotic presidential campaign with the loosest of loose cannons and an escalating political battle over the Supreme Court. The future feels uncertain, to say the least.

People generally don't thrive on uncertainty.

A few weeks ago I started receiving emails from the Trump campaign. One begins, "The Radical Left hates you, Friend." Another one reads, "These Radicals HATE you and everything you stand for."

How do you make somebody hate? It's easy — you tell them that they are hated. You convince them that somebody wants to hurt them, wants to take what is *rightfully theirs*.

Then you build on that fear. You tell them they have to fight back.

Big-city people like me — and Winston-Salem *is* "the big city" to many — are supposed to sneer at people who live in "flyover country." But I don't know anyone who does. I've only heard the claim from conservatives who graduated from Harvard and Yale. Politicos push that narrative for political gain.

Yes, some liberals make fun of small-town people sometimes — thanks a lot, Bill Maher. And some wonder at small-town attitudes that seem to reflect an unwarranted certitude.

But the truth is, rather than hate conservatives, most liberals want to *share* good things with them, like clean air and water, a decent living wage and health care. These are things we all need to thrive.

Agree or disagree, that's not hate.

I'm not trying to suggest that conservatives are unique in spreading fear to their followers. It's a tactic that's been used by politicians of all stripes, a feature of American politics since our founding. But some have turned it into an art form and a science. (Homework: Go to PBS.org and watch the one-hour documentary "Hacking Your Mind: Us vs. Them.")

And there are legitimate things to fear.

I spent more time on the phone than usual last week, talking to readers who are worried about what's going to happen next. I'm worried, too. Crisis is building upon crisis and our legislators don't seem to be doing anything to help.

Where are the helpers? Where are the blessed peacemakers?

Several mornings last week, early, I sat in the Hernon/Wills Supercollider Observatory (my back porch), watching the stars and drinking coffee. Venus is high in the east, bright enough to cast shadows. The Pleiades hover right overhead and Orion is proud in the south. Mars slides to the west, eager to join the evening sky. Through the internet, "Hearts of Space" host Stephen Hill sent me a message from 2009: "In stormy times, the wise remain calm, even when the world around them is in turmoil."

I think we're going to have to be our own peacemakers, you and me. As things get even more heated, we're going to have to remain calm. We're going to have to reject the voices that tempt us to hate and remind ourselves of the beauty and the kindness in the world. And share it.

Just like children sleeping

Oct 4, 2020

That was me standing in the field in front of Reynolda House on Thursday night, with my second-hand telescope and a couple of friends (safely distanced), waiting for the full moon to rise. It came up in the east from behind the trees right on schedule, orange-yellow, creamy and totally entrancing, for maybe half an hour before moving behind the gathering clouds.

I wasn't much aware of the moon and the stars as a kid — I liked watching TV instead. I grew up in a middle-class neighborhood — well, upper-middle-class, maybe — middle-upper-middle — we did all right — in Burlington in the 1960s and '70s, in a modern housing development on a street with other children my age. We had a fenced-in backyard and a brown mutt named Cocoa. We never wanted for anything material, my sister and me. We never worried about what we would eat or where we would sleep. When we had medical needs, "Insurance will cover it," Dad said.

I was enamored of hippies as a kid — the TV kind, with long hair and colorful clothes who said, "Groovy, man." I had an electric guitar and amp and thought I might be the next Lobo if I were just discovered by a record agent.

I thought The Monkees were better than The Beatles and today more people agree with me than did then. Prescient, me.

One of my fondest memories is of one night near Christmas time, lying on the carpeted floor near the tree, watching its lights play out intermittently against the ceiling. I felt warm and safe.

We had stability, which I think is about the best gift children could have.

Oh, there was still angst. I was as awkward and self-conscious as any kid. But even in that tumultuous age, we had stability. For most of my life, even when unemployed, there have been resources, social and financial, on which I could rely.

But things have changed in America, even putting aside the current political campaigns and health crisis. Uncertainty and gloom have been hanging in the American air. For some time our country has been experiencing what economists Anne Case and Angus Deaton call "deaths of despair" — higher rates of suicide, opioid overdoses and alcohol-related illnesses. "Something is making life worse, especially for less-educated whites," they write in "Deaths of Despair and the Future of Capitalism," published earlier this year.

In January 2019, an NBC News/Wall Street Journal poll showed that a sizable majority of Americans thought that the U.S. was headed in the wrong direction under President Trump. Asked to sum up their feelings, respondents used terms like "wrong track," "disarray," "turmoil," "polarized," "declining" and "shambles."

The funny thing is that even Trump's strongest supporters were dissatisfied with our national direction. Maybe for different reasons than everyone else.

Talk is increasing of an impending civil war, and it's unnerving — though it's a hopeful sign that those who expect it also seem to expect someone else to start it.

Maybe they'll all just sit waiting until their guns rust.

"I don't like any of this," a young woman on TikTok told me, waving her hands to signify — everything. "Don't get me wrong, I don't want to die. I want to live. But I'm just not happy with all of . . . *this*."

Sometimes I feel like that.

How did we get here, where even without a pandemic, so many have to worry about the necessities of life — food, employment, the possibility of losing their homes or going bankrupt because of a health care bill, even the likelihood of being able to retire someday with a subsistence income?

Personally, I'd point the finger all the way back to former House Speaker Newt Gingrich, who introduced the notion that compromise was overrated. I'd point to the corporate shift from providing workers with strong salaries and benefits to giving shareholders better returns. I'd point to the accompanying shift of the tax burden from the rich to the middle class, to fewer resources made available for mental health problems, to inflammatory social media.

But that's just my opinion. Yours may vary. And maybe if we talked for a few hours, we'd find some consensus.

But we all seem to agree that what we're doing now, as a society, just isn't working.

So how do we change direction?

Friday morning I got up and lit candles while I waited for the coffee to brew, creating warmth and calm in my kitchen. Then I stood on the back porch and watched the full moon play through the clouds, just below Mars. The stars, those I could see, were stable behind the clouds.

To some degree life will be uncertain no matter what we do. But if we could bring some measure of stability to our society, if we could provide more resources for those who need them, if we could turn our politics to making struggling people's lives easier rather than more difficult — it might save some lives.

Could we try it?

Of all the things I miss

Oct 18, 2020

Last Sunday morning I sat in my kitchen, drinking coffee and listening to the rain fall on leaves and gravel.

When it eased a little, the squirrel I call Charles appeared, searching for me through the screen door. I tossed him peanuts and apologized for keeping him waiting. It was a lazy morning.

Later in the day, my friend Eddie Huffman sent me a link to a song, "You Missed My Heart," the version sung by Phoebe Bridgers (written by Jimmy LaValle and Mark Kozelek). It name-checks some places we'd seen during a trip to West Virginia several years ago.

It's essentially a murder ballad, along the lines of the Louvin Brothers' "Knoxville Girl," but with an arrangement and performance so delicate that it comes across more as a tender tale of heartache, of love gone wrong. It got stuck in my head and became the soundtrack for my week.

Sunday evening, I learned that my friend Michael Renegar had died.

His death was unexpected. I'd seen him in the hospital the week before, where he was being treated for complications from diabetes, and he had been cleared to go home. But he never made it.

I first met Michael when I reviewed his first collection of

ghost stories, "Roadside Revenants," for the Journal, some — goodness, 14 years ago. He was the best storyteller I ever listened to — not because of any level of polished technique, but because of his obvious enthusiasm for the tales. Michael knew the stories cold, their histories, their rhythms and details. They were part of his heritage.

He was also one of the gentlest people I've ever met. A big man, he could get fiery online, like so many of us do, but in person, he always spoke softly. Even in the midst of his health trials, of which there were many, he usually had a smile on his face.

I wish I could have shared one more Halloween with him.

An only child, Michael was especially close to his parents. His mother, Katie Lee, died about six months ago. A day never passed that Michael didn't mourn her. And now, his elderly father, Flay, mourns him. So does his writing partner, Amy Greer; they were close enough that they called each other "Brother" and "Sis."

And in that, in being mourned, Michael is blessed. There are people who cared whether he lived or died. Not everybody has that. Not everybody gets to be someone else's favorite person.

There's a strange juxtaposition in America right now. There's so much suffering, because of the virus, because of unemployment, uncertainty, and because of prejudice. At the same time, there's so much anger — toward the people who are suffering. Some just don't want to be bothered. They want to be blithe. But since they can't be, they're angry instead. People cry out, "we're being hurt, we're being killed," and the response they hear is, "I've got everything I need, why don't you?"

A minor case came before the Supreme Court earlier this month — a sort of clean-up detail from the 2015 *Obergefell v. Hodges* decision. The Court declined to hear it, but Justice Clarence Thomas took the opportunity to assert that he thought the decision, which declared that same-sex couples have a constitutional right to marry under the 14th Amendment guarantee to equal protection of the law, had been decided wrongly. His statement made no difference to the law; it was just an opportunity to express a little spite, apparently.

Judge Amy Coney Barrett spent the week trying to assure Senate Democrats that she wasn't going to destroy people's lives, but Thomas reminded us that he's not given up yet.

Remember how same-sex marriage was supposed to bring about the end of civilization? The Bible would be labeled "hate speech" and preachers would be forced to perform gay marriages in their churches?

It's been five years and none of that has happened.

So you'd think we could move on. You'd think we'd have bigger fish to fry, like figuring out how to provide everyone with access to health care and a living wage.

But some will never give up trying to control other people's lives.

They turn to young people, LGBTQ youth, who are ostracized and bullied and, as a result, have higher-than-average rates of suicide.

Treating them with dignity is literally suicide prevention. But that would call for caring rather than condemning.

People are separated from their loved ones, behind panes of glass in hospital beds. They're desperate for touch, for comfort. The separation could have been prevented — if not by the government, by a citizenry that said, "Sure, I'll wear a mask." But.

Despite the beauty of this world, life can be harsh at times. People have to deal with its jagged edges, and it can cut them.

Anyone who can find love is blessed. Anyone who hears "I will always have your back" is blessed. Anyone who would be mourned is blessed.

Damn the people who stand in their way.

Where the pure air recognized

Dec 27, 2020

In December, I moved.

After 15 years on the edge of downtown, conditions changed in my apartment building, home of the Hernon/Wills Supercollider Observatory (my back porch), annex of Alexandria's library, refuge of squirrels and stink bugs. After a blessedly short search, my friend the Realtor found for me a modest bungalow in the historic Washington Park neighborhood. It reminded me of poet Patti Smith's century-old bungalow in Rockaway Beach, N.Y., and though that's not what convinced me, it did assure me. If a one-time resident of the Chelsea Hotel can turn a storm-ravaged bungalow in a suburban neighborhood into an art project and headquarters, maybe I can, too.

And so I walked the two flights of stairs up to my apartment about a thousand times, carrying boxes down with me on each return. I drove the main artery of Broad Street, in a moving van and a compact car, about a hundred times — sometimes at night, watching downtown and its monolith from the crest of Cascade Avenue, peering at the eerie glow of the spidery arches above the Green Street pedestrian bridge and the ghostly blue lights of the Molly Leight bridge. At night, our city is lovely.

I didn't do it all by myself; I had, and will have, plenty of help from my friends.

A house is a continuing project. As of this writing, the books aren't even back on their shelves yet. There are walls to paint and trenches to dig. I ask myself almost every day, *what am I going to do with a yard?*

One of my first acts was to rip the carpet from two rooms (with the help of my indefatigable friend, Bob Beerman). I intended to cover the floors of both rooms with some warm, high-tech flooring, but one was wooden, painted but faded blue, chipped and spackled with red and yellow. The more I looked at it, the more I liked it.

It's an honest floor. It's an artist's floor. I'm not going to cover it; I'm going to add to its scars.

It's not easy to leave downtown. For decades now it's been one of the defining factors in my life. I've had the luxury of walking to work almost daily — as well as to a library, a bookstore, restaurants, entertainment venues. Walking through the arts district recently, I thought about people I used to know, places I used to frequent: The Garage; Urban Artware; Mary's Gourmet Diner; and, a few times, empty storefronts appropriated (mostly legally) for artistic performances.

People in their 20s and 30s experience a different downtown than that of my friends and me. But our downtown still represents a cohesive community vision of creativity.

My new neighborhood — a working-class neighborhood whose streets are lined with pickup trucks and SUVs as well as a Prius here and there — is artful in its own way. I walk its streets admiring architecture, gardens, stonework, decorations — especially the cheerful Christmas decorations that light the night. I hope my neighbors keep them up for another month or so. In fact, maybe they should be refreshed every few weeks until the pandemic is over, or just always.

A couple of Sundays ago some neighbors sponsored a food drive and I stopped by to drop off some cans, pet a few dogs, greet some friends and Journal letter writers. This is a warm, accepting place.

I wonder how it will change me. I'm sure it will. New habits will be adopted, new associations formed, new influences felt.

I wonder about the wildlife; if I'll see the nocturnal foxes and possums that surely live here. Will I lure the crows from the light pole across the street to my front porch?

I'll let you know.

Even as I'm settling in, I'm aware that others are fighting right now to keep their homes — and some have lost. It's a massive failure of our institutions that they have to struggle with housing during a pandemic.

I won't forget them. And I won't take my home for granted.

Friday brings my favorite holiday: New Year's Day. The world will sit still for a few minutes as we re-calibrate. At least, that's how I imagine it. The sun and the Earth — they don't know our calendars. They just keep moving, the invisible rubber band of gravity pulling and pushing them closer and farther.

We're the ones who assign meaning to their dance, the meaning of renewal, of hope. I'm down with that. Hey: We made it through that horrible 2020. *We made it.*

For the new year, take these words from a Buddhist prayer I learned a decade ago: May you be free of fear; may you be at ease; may you be happy.

See you next year.

From the mountains of faith
to a river so deep

Feb 7, 2021

Following the violent attack on the Capitol on Jan. 6, some media outlets and religious scholars have turned an eye onto the Christian nationalism that contributed to the chaos. Apparently, many of the insurrectionists were motivated by a militant strain of Christianity that has bonded with misguided patriotism to create a dangerous and destructive theology.

The FBI has warned that we can expect similar incidents in the future, especially as some Christian nationalists continue to hold hands with QAnon supporters and white supremacists.

In essence, Christian nationalism teaches that America is meant to be, preeminently, a Christian nation; that you can't be a good American unless you're a good Christian.

Some people buried in Arlington National Cemetery would like to discuss that with you, gents.

So would other Christians with broader minds.

And though it's not a belief that always leads to violence — some are content to simply plead their case — the militants among them are certain that their actions are mandated by God. That fervor makes them even more dangerous.

I remember when I first heard the claim that America was a Christian nation. It was explained to me when I was a teen, by a minister I considered to be my mentor. But even though I respected him, the teaching didn't sit well with me for a number of reasons.

One was that I'd not heard it before. It wasn't part of my church's doctrine.

I grew up in one of those small sects that believed we were the One True Church and everybody else got it wrong — like, you know, thousands of other One True Churches. In this particular One True Church, the salvation of figures, from the Rev. Billy Graham to the Rev. Martin Luther King Jr., was not only questioned, but outright denied. They weren't "real" Christians. Yet suddenly I was supposed to accept that men like James Madison and Alexander Hamilton, whose names I'd never heard in church, were acting on our behalf.

Were they part of our fellowship? Or were they honorary Christians?

It also didn't sit well with me because, though I hadn't yet heard the word "disenfranchise," I knew that the claim that this nation was *mine, ours,* would suggest that my classmates at school were, in some fashion, less than me. It seemed an arrogant claim, and one that probably wouldn't go over very well if I tried to explain it to them.

But mostly, the claim didn't sit well with me because, as an avid Bible reader, I knew that Jesus had never asked for a nation. There was no biblical prophecy: "And your ancestors shall travel over the sea and come to a land . . . . " There was no command for his followers to form a government. In fact, when people brought up any kind of politics with Jesus — either to bait him or bribe him — he tended to reply with phrases like, "My kingdom is not of this earth." The Great Commission he gave his disciples was, "Go into every nation and preach the Gospel," not, "Go into every nation and preach a nation."

And when he told his followers what kind of life to expect, it wasn't one of ownership, of privilege and power, but one of persecution. They would be "in the world but not of the world." He never envisioned a time when his followers would be in charge of an earthly kingdom. It just wasn't there.

I realize there's a popular interpretation that connects the dots between various muddy biblical passages to reach other conclusions. They see America in this interpretation.

But those confusing passages have been interpreted in a

variety of ways over the last two centuries. It seems overly confident to conclude that *this* is the interpretation that finally gets it right.

I have no doubt that many proponents of a Christian America are acting from a pure impulse: They want our nation to be righteous, to follow teachings they see as righteous.

But there are also those, including some in government, who are seeking an advantage that no one else is afforded. To declare this a Christian nation is to declare a place of prominence for one group that is denied other citizens, based solely on religion.

On its surface, that seems contrary to every constitutional principle we know.

And it makes me wonder what the plan is for those excluded: Are they to be coerced to believe things against their conscience? Are they to accept being relegated to a lower status?

Americans will never all agree on religion; it's one of those basic factors that drives divisions between us if we let it. But you'd think the fact that the Constitution guarantees us the freedom to follow the dictates of religious conscience rather than enforced dogma is something that we could celebrate and honor.

It's a blessing that many others throughout the world never receive.

That ice is slowly melting

Feb 21, 2021

It was a block of seltzer water cans — my most destructive vice these days — that froze the register. I rocked on my heels while waiting for the big box store's busy attendant to make her way to me.

"I think I scanned it twice," I told her, with a little irritation in my voice.

"What did you do that for?" she asked. For the slightest instant I bristled, but then I saw the crinkles around her eyes and knew they were matched by a smile under her mask. I had to laugh.

"I guess I just didn't have anything better to do."

That happened a couple weeks ago. I kept thinking about the exchange throughout the day and chuckling. It's not the sort of wit that'll get you on Jimmy Kimmel, but it lifted my mood a bit.

You know that little gizmo with the hydraulic thingamajig that gently glides your front door shut? It's called a door closer, but I didn't know that when mine broke last week.

I took its parts to the hardware store and approached a clerk, who asked, "What can I do for you?"

"I need one of these," I said, extending my hands.

"Well, do you want one that's already broken or would you like to break it yourself?"

Again, I had to laugh. "I guess I could break it myself."

Neither of these workers was trying to be a smart aleck. They were just free and relaxed and ready to introduce a little humor into the pandemic-dimmed lives of their customers. Every little bit helps.

Incidentally, neither here nor there: "The customer is always right" is a terrible philosophy, especially when dealing with front-line workers. Who handle, say, your food.

There have been a few similar incidents in recent days that just left me feeling good. They've been an effective balance to the occasional sobs and the bouts of anger and frustration that manifest themselves over the tiniest things. We're making our way. We're adjusting. And if you're like me, you sense a curve in the road ahead.

In the paper, I keep seeing hints of recovery, or at least improvement. Our COVID numbers are starting to go down. One day last week there were no new deaths to report in Forsyth County. And rather than argue over whether we should get the vaccine, people are now arguing over who should get it first.

Some haven't looked deeply enough to understand the wisdom of inoculating prisoners — it helps keep prison staff healthy, too, and their families. Still, and maybe I'm overly optimistic to say so, but I think it's a healthy debate. Yes, let's argue about who gets it first, all the way until everyone who wants to be inoculated has been inoculated. That's a worthwhile discussion.

One morning last week I found myself humming as I left for work. As I started my car, I realized that I was in a good mood — for no clearly discernible reason. Nothing special had happened; it was just a good day so far.

On the road, I start listing things for which I feel grateful, just for the fun of it.

> *I have a reliable car. With a heater and intermit-*
> *tent wipers.*
> *I have a fuzzy blanket with the face of a fox*
> *stenciled onto it.*
> *I have a jar of cashews that my friend roasted*
> *and gave to me.*
> *Three new spacecraft have just arrived at Mars.*

There are castles.
After work, I can go home and read.
If the sky is clear tonight, I'll be able to see the
crescent moon.

Overall, these last few weeks, the world seems to have faded from an angry orange to a more placid blue. I can't quite put my finger on why. But I'm grateful.

I'm not Pollyannaish enough to think that everything works out for the best — it doesn't, for many. Life can be disappointing, painful, harsh.

But sometimes the fates smile upon us, the background music swells and the traffic lights all turn green. And I recall what Jack Kerouac wrote in "The Dharma Bums": ". . . though the flesh be bugged, the circumstances of existence are pretty glorious."

Some keep their eyes open for those circumstances and the moments in which they appear. Some keep them stocked in memory, for later use. Some try to generate those moments for other people.

One day recently I ordered take-out from a downtown restaurant, and while I was waiting, I noticed the cashier, who was wearing a head covering and a mask. When she brought my order, I told her, "I hope you don't mind my saying so, but you have beautiful eyes."

"Thanks," she said, "I grew them myself."

Let's go down, come on down

Apr 11, 2021

It was a rainy March day and it was time for a driveabout, so I threw a heavy jacket into the car and headed northwest.

Up N.C. 67 through East Bend, I took the turn that leads across the mighty, muddy Yadkin River and stopped at the Rockford General Store to fuel up on candy. The lady behind the counter and I greeted each other through our masks.

"How's business?" I asked.

"Slower than usual, but not bad," she said.

I wound up with two bags drawn from the store's big glass jars: one for chocolates, the other for Cherry Sours and Red Hots — which, I learned, don't actually go together as well as one might think. But they kept me alert.

The rain had tapered off, but the air was still cool, so I donned my jacket and strolled through the concrete and crumbling brick of Rockford Park, built among the remnants of an old hotel, the town's own little Bayon temple.

Back in the car, I was surprised to find that I could pick up WDAV from Davidson. I'm a WFDD devotee, but it was a day, not for commentary, but for Rachel Stewart and Mozart Café.

North then, on winding two-lane roads, turning north at every intersection, slowly around the steep curves, further north, as I rolled past tractors, tobacco barns, brightly painted houses, fields, fences, turkeys, cows, crosses, flags. At one point I came across somebody's goats, making a run for it.

Go, goats, go.

Before long, the vista opened up and there were the mountains, blue in the distance.

Eventually, I lost the station. While playing radio roulette, I landed on the plaintive folk spiritual that goes:

> *O sisters let's go down*
> *Let's go down, come on down*
> *O sisters let's go down*
> *Down in the river to pray*

Further north, I crossed the Virginia state line, then the unmistakable ribbon of the Blue Ridge Parkway. Eventually I reached U.S. 58, turned east, and meandered through Stuart and Martinsville, winding up in Danville.

I parked near the farmer's market in the river district, asplash with former tobacco warehouses and cobblestone streets, where people were lining up to be inoculated, and walked across the pedestrian bridge that spans the Dan River, pausing to watch huge tree limbs being washed downstream by that morning's rain.

Standing above the Dan, usually shallow and bright, but now swollen to match the Yadkin in volume and color, I thought about a song from my childhood, sung by The Wilburn Brothers:

> *Roll muddy river, roll on muddy river, roll on*
> *I've got a notion you'll go to the ocean alone*
> *I've got a baby in Tennessee*
> *who's long been awaitin' for little ol' me*
> *Roll, muddy river, roll on, muddy river, roll on*

Back on the south side of the river, the paved multi-purpose trail led me toward an antique mall I knew, with two floors full of junk and treasures. The last time I was there, the proprietor and I ran into each other in an aisle. We both pulled our masks up and she, gesturing to hers, said, "These are crazy times, aren't they?"

"Yeah, they sure are," I agreed.

The mall was closed; the building vacated.

I looked around, hoping someone would come up and explain this to me.

No one did.

As I walked up Main Street, everyone I passed wore a mask. They seem to be taking the virus seriously in Danville.

I thought about the skeptics who believe this, a worldwide phenomenon that has taken millions of lives, all to be some scheme, some elaborate theater for some ill-defined purpose. Who benefits, mask-makers?

Does it ever cross their minds that they could be wrong? Look at all the other things they're wrong about.

The end of our COVID era will come, eventually, but not all at once. There will be no grand pronouncements, no declarations. It'll end with fits and starts, with tragic flare-ups here and there, now and then. We may need our masks, intermittently, for some time to come.

Eventually, some will claim that we over-compensated. We panicked. We didn't have to do all that.

To which I say: good. We *should* over-compensate. We should take *ridiculous* precautions.

Because if you don't want to fall off a building, you don't stand on a ledge and dare the wind to push you.

After wandering around a little more, it was time to go home. I drove past the historic houses on Main Street, took U.S. 29 to Reidsville, U.S. 158 to here.

With my chocolates almost gone, I ran by the grocery store. In the aisles, as I passed other shoppers, we caught each other's eyes and nodded. A little nod to civility. To good will. To good health.

We'll pull this country through to safety — kicking and screaming, if we have to. But we'll do it. We'll cross that river and meet on the other shore.

Them that's got shall have

May 23, 2021

There was a little boy named Roland Rogers, 9 years old. He lived with his father, Robert; his older sister, Rita; and her 1-year-old son, Ryan, all in a small but costly apartment.

Rita took Roland to school, where the teacher gave him a sheet with some writing on it that he couldn't read. He was pointed to a seat and he sat. He tried listening to the teacher, but she didn't make much sense, and all the other kids were just talking, anyway. So Roland took out his pencil and drew a cartoon.

Eventually school let out and Roland stood on the street until Rita arrived and took him home. There, he drew some more — he liked drawing foxes — while listening to his father and sister talk about money.

They had an EBT card. They had to get a bus pass, they had to pay the bills, they had to get groceries. They split up the chores and the money and hoped they could get it all done.

It just confused Roland.

The next day, Rita took Roland back to school, where he sat by himself, drawing. No one spoke to him.

The days passed like that for a month. Roland faced each moment with a degree of helpless resignation mingled with an undercurrent of fear. He felt as if there was a stone in his stomach. Then it was over.

I know about Roland because I was him for an hour.

A couple weeks ago I participated in a "poverty simulation" during a day of activities organized by Leadership Winston-Salem. It's essentially — "game" isn't the right word, it's not a frivolous thing, but it's essentially a role-playing game in which some 70 participants took on other identities — people of various ages, genders, backgrounds and ethnicities and more individual characteristics — Roland had a learning disability — and, with meager resources, tried to make ends meet. For an hour, everyone hustled from one "station" — home, store, work, bank, social services — to another, hoping to get everything done. A lot of time was spent standing in line.

The simulation is an eye-opener. For me, it reaffirmed something that many of us already know: Being poor is expensive — and exhausting. You've got the money to take the bus to the job interview, but you may not make it to the utility office before it closes. If you miss a payment, the heat is turned off and there's a fee to turn it back on. You can't pay the car registration until payday, so you get a ticket that you also have to pay. You can get a payday loan, but that means you'll have less on payday. And the rent just went up.

An hour was long enough to get the point: Anyone who muses about poor people lounging around at home after cashing their cushy welfare checks just doesn't know what the hell they're talking about.

Roland lingered with me for several days, reminding me of childhood feelings of unspoken anxiety and vulnerability. Even with generally happy childhoods like mine, I'll bet many of us have experienced those feelings. Maybe sharply. Maybe persistently.

Most of us receive support and love and develop resilience. Time passes and we wake to new days and new feelings. And as we grow up, we forget how fragile children can be.

The other day, I came across a tweet:

> *So I took my daughter to Barnes & Noble and I told her I wanted a parent book about child anxiety.*
> *I started skimming through it and found a page titled: Alone at school.*

I looked at her and asked her if that's her and she nodded yes. I tried to hold back my tears.

I tried to hold back mine.

Did you see that little 10-year-old Palestinian girl on TV last week, surrounded by rubble? Her name is Nadine Abdel-Taif and she lives in Gaza.

"I can't do anything," she says. "I am only 10, what am I supposed to do? Fix it? I'm only 10. I just want to be a doctor, or anything, to help my people, but I can't. I'm just a kid."

I don't care about the politics. Nadine deserves better. Roland deserves better. Every kid does.

Who's going to fix it?

There are people who try to help: parents, counselors, even politicians. One of them, a very prominent figure, has instituted a child tax credit to give working families more resources for their kids.

Others are in the schools, listening to them and assuring them, "I believe in you." Some in our state legislature want to force these others to be spies and tattle-tales, as if that would help.

They won't be, I guarantee.

People who try to help should be recognized. You tell me who they are. I'll tell everyone else.

Filled with light and air

Jun 6, 2021

My favorite song was the anthemic "Free Electric Band," by Albert Hammond, and the AM station we listened to played it about once every two hours. In between, we heard Neil Young's "Heart of Gold," Argent's "Hold Your Head Up," "Papa Was a Rolling Stone" by The Temptations, "Day by Day" from the musical "Godspell" and this weird thing called "Take a Walk on the Wild Side," which everyone thought was terrible.

We still listened to it, though, and sensed that Lou Reed knew something we didn't.

We'd lay blankets out in the yard, seven or eight neighborhood kids and me, and sit on them, tanning ourselves (*on purpose*), listening to the radio and drinking Coke and Dr. Pepper.

For my birthday I received a canvas tent, which I set up in the backyard with ropes leading from the poles to the metal stakes, about 2 feet out. My friends and I camped out there once or twice a month. We'd sit up late shining our flashlights, devouring potato chips and making up ghost stories that always ended with a jump: "Who took my bloody toe? YOU DID!" Then in the morning we'd wake up piled on top of each other like little fox cubs, victims of gravity and the yard's slope.

Some afternoons I'd lounge in my tent, the scent of hot canvas in the air, and read comic books like "Korak, Son of

Tarzan," with Frank Thorne's fine-line depictions of hideous lizard men and lithesome waifs who needed rescuing. I had a stack of paperbacks about the adventures of Doc Savage — a superhuman overachiever — and read about one a day. They were truly awful, written in a rush by hacks under a house name for a penny a word without the benefit of a second draft, but I thrilled to them. I hadn't yet discovered Jules Verne or Robert E. Howard.

This is what summer was like when I was a kid growing up in Burlington.

I didn't know anything about the Vietnam War or Richard Nixon. "Look at Mother Nature on the run" was just a song lyric. The season felt eternal, and returning to school every fall was a shock. Where did the time go?

Now, the summer heat feels like being broiled. Some years I experience a sort of reverse of the seasonal affective disorder that afflicts some people in the winter. The heat is just too oppressive and it brings me down.

I'm not alone, I know.

Even before the pandemic, medical authorities were citing a mental health crisis in America, with too many people struggling against feelings of anxiety and despair, reflected in growing suicide rates and opioid addictions.

The pandemic did nothing to ease the situation. According to a survey conducted by the Harris Poll in late February, 1 in 5 adults reported that their mental health has worsened over the past year. Parents of young children, essential workers, young people, low-income populations and people of color have been especially hard hit.

On top of that, a new study published in JAMA Psychiatry says that more than 30% of COVID survivors may have developed PTSD.

Sometimes I wonder why everybody doesn't have PTSD. Then sometimes I think everybody does.

We're recovering — in increments. One day the full staff in a café near my house was wearing masks — the next, none were. Which is fine; they've all been vaccinated. I'm still carrying my mask, and I admit, it's not because I need it — I've been vaccinated, too — but because I don't want to be the first jerk to show his face when no one else is.

Hey, I'm not the one who started hefting moral and political weight onto a public-health crisis.

But, as always, there are comforts to help us cope, if we just look for them. My backyard is shady, morning and late afternoon, and there's plenty of room for a tent. My birdseed brings all the birds to the yard — cardinals, robins, bluebirds. In the evening, there are swarms of fireflies.

Next on my reading list is John Hood's "Mountain Folks," and its cover copy makes it look like a hoot.

My friends and I put away our masks when we meet and we've just about remembered how to carry on a conversation. My bike tires are full of air and there's this roadside stop, Ben's Ice Cream, outside Eagle Springs on N.C. 211 — it's worth a trip.

Let's keep checking in with each other, OK?

The summer of 2021 can't be like the summer of 1972. But it won't be like the summer of 2020, either.

Tall white mansions
and little shacks

Jun 20, 2021

During my obsessive social media scrolling last week, I came across a clip of a TV commentator winding down a conversation with two panelists about critical race theory:

"First of all, doctor, your counter is predicated on the idea that there's a one-on-one relationship between critical race theory and critical theory as sort of produced from the Marxist tradition, from the Frankfort school, etc., when in fact, critical race theory has, certainly, connections to any kind of critical, intellectual discourse, but it's also connected to critical legal studies, which was not committed to sort of inheriting all of the kind of Gramscian and Marxian sort of ideas that you're talking about. . . ."

So on and so forth.

If you waded through that, you may have a future in academia.

My conversations tend to be more along the lines of, "Did you like the movie? Yeah, me, too. I remembered that one guy from that other movie."

But the man with the scholarly approach was Marc Lamont Hill, Ph.D., and I don't know a single thing about him except that he knows more about critical race theory than me — and more than any of the legislators who have been busy filing bills to forbid teaching CRT or "The 1619 Project" or anything else racially controversial in public schools — including our own Sen. Thom Tillis.

The funny thing is, in many cases, they're forbidding the teaching of something that no public school is teaching. You may as well file bills prohibiting possums from buying houses.

This is, as should be clear from Hill's soliloquy, a graduate-level topic.

So why are *we* talking about it?

Because Republicans, losing at the voting booth, need a wedge issue. They need something to rile up the voters. "President Biden is a dookie head" isn't working. Neither is persecuting LGBTQ youth.

Smart people tell me that this one is a winner.

Across the country, local school boards are being confronted with angry parents demanding, "Don't you dare teach that thing you don't teach!" Thankfully, that embarrassing madness hasn't yet reached Winston-Salem/Forsyth County Schools.

Incidentally, the bills that Republicans are filing, besides being based on nothing, are also filled with sketchy, hard-to-enforce language, some of which clearly violates the First Amendment. "Most legal scholars say that these bills impinge on the right to free speech and will likely be dismissed in court," Adam Harris wrote in The Atlantic last month.

So that'll cost their constituents some tax money.

And they're using their criticism of critical race theory as a springboard to criticize other conversations about race, in board rooms and the military as well as in schools.

The supporters of these bills are framing pretty much any conversation about race *that originates with Black people* as racist attempts to say that white people are inferior. So they get to dump on both minorities and education while pretending to defend equality.

Here's the thing: I'm a son of the South. I grew up in the 1960s and '70s around people who took it as an article of faith that Black people were innately inferior to white people. It was in the water. I couldn't borrow a cup of sugar from the guy up the street from me without hearing about it.

Some of the people who espoused these things were good people, *religious* people. They didn't hate African Americans;

they had compassion for people they saw as intellectually and morally inferior.

And maybe that's the best they could do, given the systemic culture in which they were raised.

But how ironic is it that the descendants of those people are now afraid that schools might teach that *they* are inferior?

For some, this might elicit a little empathy toward our African American friends and neighbors who had to endure just that kind of attitude.

Instead, it elicits fevered, angry, misinformed activism.

Despite the absence of critical race theory in public schools, race and discrimination are sometimes discussed there in straightforward and respectful terms. They need to be. "African American history," Winston-Salem/Forsyth County Schools board member Elisabeth Motsinger tells me, "is American history." She's right. Black and white lives have been intertwined since before this nation began. We rise and fall together.

Distorting those conversations and stirring up anger and fear for political gain may be a winner at the voting booth — but it shouldn't be. We should all know better by now than to take the bait.

What have you done for me lately?

Jul 18, 2021

Who else was thrilled when Zaila Avant-garde won the 2021 Scripps National Spelling Bee?

I first learned about this remarkable 14-year-old girl when a brief clip of her victory appeared on my Twitter feed last weekend. There she was, joking about Bill Murray's possible connection to the challenging word "murraya," then, a few seconds later, leaping into the air, exuberant beyond containment. I don't think I've ever seen a smile that wide. I watched it over and over again.

I later learned that this Louisiana native is a bit of a nerd; she juggles. She's also an accomplished athlete who plays on her school's basketball team.

Following her victory, she's been offered countless college scholarships. Her future looks bright.

She told The Associated Press that she'd like to inspire other African American spelling bee hopefuls, particularly those who might not be able to afford the lessons needed to be competitive.

Oh, yeah, the young lady is African American, and only the second Black child to ever win this particular competition.

Zaila's story is in sharp contrast to another that came to my attention just the day before — that of a Tennessee parents' organization that hopes to use the new controversy over critical race theory to prevent students from learning about a 6-year-old African American girl named Ruby Bridges.

Ruby was the first Black child to attend an all-white primary school in Louisiana, in November 1960, to a cacophonous background of violent, racist insults flung by white folks. Four federal marshals were required to make sure she wasn't attacked.

The leader of the parents' group objects to books about Ruby being included in the school curriculum, arguing that "the mention of 'a large crowd of angry white people who didn't want Black children in a white school' too harshly delineated between Black and white people, and . . . didn't offer 'redemption' at its end."

In other words, they don't think children — white children — can handle the truth if it doesn't have a happy ending.

That, to me, summarizes the recent Republican efforts to control what teachers can teach our children about race. If there's a chance that it might make white children uncomfortable — well, we can't have that.

No, our kids should only hear about Zaila.

Not too long ago I received a letter from a reader who identified himself as "A Patriot." He wanted to make sure I knew that the "slave states, Jim Crow laws, the KKK etc were all Democratic."

Yes, he's right; Democrats were behind much of the racism our country suffered before the 1960s.

Some Republicans stop the story there, but that's only the first part. What happened next was that a majority of Republicans *and* Democrats passed the Civil Rights Act of 1964, a bill that was written by a Democrat and signed into law by a Democratic president.

What happened next was that the Republican Party adopted a Southern strategy of subtle racism to appeal to disaffected Democrats, who changed their party allegiance.

What happened next was Willie Horton and welfare queens.

What happened next was Republican strategist Lee Atwater's confession of dog-whistle politics, revealed after his untimely 1991 death. ("You start out in 1954 by saying, 'N-----, n-----, n-----.' By 1968 you can't say 'n-----' — that hurts you, backfires. So you say stuff like, uh, forced busing, states' rights, and all that stuff, and you're getting so abstract.")

Today, instead of saying, "They're going to steal our jobs," Republican strategists are saying, "They're going to teach our children to feel guilty for being white."

And they do so while trying to portray themselves as champions of race relations.

Look it: In Congress, 83% of racial and ethnic minority members are Democrats compared to 17% Republican. Which party is committed to racial diversity?

Which party's members take offense from Black people just asserting that their lives *matter*?

And which party defends Confederate portraits and monuments?

None of this is to say that all Republicans are racists — nor would I say that all racists are Republicans. There are Democrats who harbor hateful attitudes. I truly believe that most Americans oppose racism — though some understand what it is better than others.

I'll always respect President George W. Bush for appointing African Americans like Gen. Colin Powell and Condoleezza Rice to high ranks in his administration. Sen. Mitt Romney has a warm spot in my heart for marching with Black Lives Matter protesters in 2020.

But when Sen. Ted Cruz complains that critical race theory "is every bit as racist as the klansmen in white sheets" — well, I just want to get him on record as opposing klansmen in white sheets, because I didn't know that was his position.

And when our Republican state legislators make an issue of critical race theory — *which isn't even taught in North Carolina schools* — and draw up a list of concepts that teachers are forbidden from teaching — *which none of them are teaching* — I see nothing but another race-baiting attempt to scare up votes.

It's long past time that people of good will stop taking the bait.

With velvet roses
digging freedom flight

Aug 1, 2021

It was about 3:21 a.m. when I gave up and got up.

It's an age thing. It just happens sometimes.

The air in the house felt a little stale, so when the coffee was ready, I took a cup onto the front porch to see what the early morning looks like in my neighborhood. There was a soft, cool breeze. A few stars blinked above. Traffic shushed along about a mile away. All else was quiet when this fox came prancing silently up the road. She was small and delicate, with short, sleek, very deep-red summer fur melting into black stockings.

She stopped and we looked at each other.

"Hello," she said.

"Hello," I replied.

Then she walked over to the sidewalk and sat primly.

"You're new here, aren't you?" she asked.

"I moved in about six months ago."

"Ah."

"Do you live nearby?" I asked.

"Two hills up that way," she said, swinging her white muzzle toward the north. "I've been here for a couple of litters. Have you by any chance seen a little kit wandering around? He's about, oh, yea high." She held a paw about a foot in the air.

"No, sorry, I haven't. Is he lost?"

She bunched her shoulders up and released them, exhaling.

"No, I'm sure he's around somewhere. He just gets a little ahead of himself sometimes."

"Kids," I said.

"Yes. I've got three this year. There's the biggest one, and believe me, he's a little whirlwind. There's his smaller brother, who just wants to do everything he does. And their sister. I'm a little worried about her. She's so gentle, she doesn't even want to eat a bug. Do you have any kits?"

"Me? No, it's just me."

"I see."

"I haven't seen you before," I said.

"Yes, well. We foxes decided some time ago that it would be a good idea to avoid people if we could. No offense intended."

"None taken. I feel the same way sometimes."

"I don't really know all of you, of course. There are a lot of you. Some of you are very nice. But some . . ."

"Not so nice."

"And, I don't know, but you seem to rush around a lot. You're always running from your house to your . . . your little houses with those . . ." She drew a circle in the air.

"Cars?"

"'Cars.' Yes, you just rush around a lot. Except for the diggers."

"Diggers?"

She looked toward the ground and made a waving motion.

"Gardeners?"

"'Gardeners.' Yes. They seem thoughtful. Calm."

"I think they are."

"My mother was telling me once that *her* mother told her and *her* mother told her that all of this used to be forest. Well, things change."

"They do."

She turned her head toward the top of a telephone pole and I saw that a crow was sitting there.

"Hey," the crow said.

"Hello," she said.

"Everything OK?" He seemed to incline his head toward me.

"Everything's fine," she answered.

"OK, well, I'll be around." And he flew off.

"So you get along with crows?" I asked.

"Well, some of them. I know that one. We get along with cats and dogs, too."

"No kidding?"

"Some of them are a lot of fun to play with. I don't know why people seem to think we're going to bite them or something. I've never bitten anyone. I don't know *any* fox who's ever bitten anyone."

"I try to tell people that."

"You do?"

"Yeah. I tell them that you're no threat, you're not going to attack anyone. You're just trying to make your way in the world, like anyone else."

"Well . . . thanks."

"But I never knew you could talk."

She grinned. "We like to keep that quiet, you know."

"Of course."

"Well, I'm just a chatterbox this morning. I should be going," she said, standing. "Nice talking to you."

"You, too."

As she walked away, I called: "Hey, do you have a name?"

She stopped and looked back. "Not so much a name as a scent."

"A scent?"

"Yes. My family would call me something like . . . 'the one who smells like strawberries and beetles.'"

"Oh, I see. I'm Mick."

She smiled. Then she was gone.

I walked back inside and sat in my reading chair. I closed my eyes for a second and thought, *how little we know*. Next thing I knew, I was waking up to sunlight.

When I leave the rest behind

Aug 15, 2021

The three greatest pilgrimages on the planet are the Camino de Santiago — the 600-mile trek through Spain and France in the footsteps of St. James; the Hajj — the once-in-a-lifetime journey to holy Mecca; and the drive to Ben's Ice Cream in Eagle Springs, N.C.

Well . . . OK, not really. But thanks to recent readings and musings, I had those other notable journeys in mind when I finally decided to return to Ben's.

Ben's Ice Cream is a little roadside attraction I stumbled across some 15 years ago while on my way home from a golf exhibition in Southern Pines. Owned by the family that owns the adjacent Kalawi Farm, it's been making and selling its own ice cream for gosh knows how long. It's only about 90 minutes away from here, and along the way are a few very cute little towns worth exploring.

I wouldn't drive 90 minutes *just* for ice cream. Probably.

There's no need to get there early unless you want to have ice cream for breakfast, so I left my home in Washington Park around 10 a.m. Saturday, planning to meander.

I took I-40 east to I-74, then, just south of Asheboro, switched to the two-lane Business 220, which is much more interesting than the highway. I paused in tiny Star to check the condition of the spookiest house I've ever seen, a block off Main Street, an abandoned Victorian with tall gables that looks like a set from "Dark Shadows."

I wish I could show you pictures, but nature has now overgrown it, too thickly for comfortable exploration, especially during tick season.

A little further south in Biscoe, I detoured onto N.C. Highway 24 to have a peek at Troy, where I wasted half an hour in a flea market. No fox knickknacks, alas. The small town has a comic book store, though, a sure sign of intelligent life.

In Candor, I turned east onto N.C. Highway 211 and drove 5 more miles.

Ben's hasn't changed much since the last time I was there. It consists of four or five wooden structures, depending on how you count them, including a log cabin and an extensive produce stand.

The specialty is peaches: several different varieties as well as peach jam and peach salsa.

The ground is covered with the kind of sand and pine needles that I associate with the eastern part of the state. There are picnic tables, swings and a playground.

The temperature was a comfortable and surprising 72 degrees and the place was fairly crowded with mostly mask-wearing families.

There are many ice cream flavors including peach, strawberry, cherry, vanilla and various chocolates. I chose banana for my first scoop, in a cup, and sat on one of the creaky porch swings.

The fruit flavor was obvious but not overbearing. It wasn't too sweet or rich; it was light and delicious.

My next scoop was pineapple and I got it on a giant sugar cone. It was just as enjoyable.

Dessert was chocolate peanut butter.

Honestly, I could have eaten more, but I didn't want to make myself sick.

While letting the ice cream settle, I talked with a couple of ladies at a table near me. "We come here every weekend," one of them told me, "unless we go to Charlotte."

"What do you go to Charlotte for?" I asked.

"Everything except ice cream," the other one said, and they both laughed. There are no bookstores near Eagle Springs, they explained, no movie theaters.

But there's no Ben's Ice Cream in Charlotte.

Access to I-74 was close by, so the journey home was quick.

My trip to Ben's wasn't a real pilgrimage, of course, but it was a nice respite from the daily grind, from news and COVID.

A pilgrimage is, essentially, a prolonged journey taken to a specific destination in order to reach a particular goal, maybe to visit a shrine or meet an obligation. In literature, common elements include challenging obstacles, extended solitude, mysterious strangers and, after trials, enlightenment. It often has religious or mystical connotations, but that's not essential.

The pilgrim hopes that the privations of the journey, along with the effort put forth to reach the goal, will lead to a transformation, as fire purges the sword of the steel's imperfections.

I sense there's a true pilgrimage or two in my future.

Sometimes I wish America would take a pilgrimage. The goal might be greater understanding and national unity.

We've certainly had the challenges of a pilgrimage these last few years. But as a nation, we don't seem to have experienced any positive transformation — no increase in humility or wisdom. No enlightenment, no grace earned or given. Instead, I sometimes sense an increase in cruelty and arrogance, almost a determination among some to be abrasive.

That's not the pilgrim's path. We took a wrong turn somewhere.

Come with me, America. Let's find the right way together. I'll buy you an ice cream.

Sky of blackness and sorrow

Sep 12, 2021

Twenty years later, here's what I remember:

I was driving to work when the radio announcer said something about an airplane crashing into one of the twin towers of the World Trade Center. It sounded like an accident.

By afternoon, we knew enough that I closed the office and went to give blood.

Days later, CBS anchorman Dan Rather apologized to David Letterman for breaking down on his show. Letterman placed his hand over Rather's: "You're a professional, but good Christ, you're a human being."

Days later, musicians gathered for "America: A Tribute to Heroes," a benefit concert to raise money for 9/11 first responders and their families. Bruce Springsteen sang "My City of Ruins" in a candle-lit room with a group of back-up singers who exhibited the solemnity of a church choir performing penance.

> *There is a blood red circle*
> *On the cold dark ground*
> *And the rain is falling down*
> *The church door's thrown open*
> *I can hear the organ's song*

But the congregation's gone
My city of ruins
My city of ruins

People from countries around the world mourned with us; with its favored child, the most hopeful and prosperous. Some, from lands where such things happened more regularly, said, "You're one of us now."

We slowly began to learn why this had happened. Some madman named Osama bin Laden was trying to lure the U.S. into military entanglement in the Middle East. That would make it appear to the Muslims of the world that the U.S. wanted to wage war on them, bin Laden reasoned.

But we're too smart for that, I thought.

Bin Laden also wanted to stoke fear in the hearts of Americans, we heard. He wanted us to think that such an attack could happen anytime and anywhere.

But we're too smart for that, I thought.

I've since had to reassess.

I remember a grainy black-and-white photograph in some news magazine of a tough, young New Yorker confronting another tough, young New Yorker in Islamic attire, ready to pummel him, while a crowd looked on. It seemed absurd. That guy didn't have anything to do with 9/11.

I remember in 2010, a group of Muslims, including Feisal Abdul Rauf, a New York imam who had once been described by provocateur Glenn Beck as "one of the good Muslims," tried to build a community center not too far from the rubble of the twin towers. It was named "Cordoba House," after a Spanish city famous in the eighth century for the relative harmony between the Jews, Christians and Muslims who lived there.

Opponents — including Beck — foamed at the mouth, calling it the "Ground Zero Mosque," an "insult" and a "house of evil."

Life went on. We formed families and built industries, found new things to argue about. We sang and danced and shared books. We traveled and dreamed and urged the next generation to save us from ourselves.

But in the background, in the next room, someone still sang: *my city of ruins.*

Refugees came here, fleeing the violence. They took jobs, rented houses and made friends. My neighbors fed me savory dishes with names I couldn't pronounce. When my truck died, they offered me the use of their car.

For a time, I drove refugee families from the airport to their new homes in the Piedmont Triad, one small link in a life-saving chain. If I never do anything else useful with my life, I've done that.

Last weekend, The Guardian reported: "The U.S. government acted quickly after 9/11 to prevent further attacks by Islamic extremists in the U.S. . . . But while the FBI, CIA, police and the newly created Department of Homeland Security scoured the country and the world for radicalized Muslims, an existing threat was overlooked — white supremacist extremists already in the U.S., whose numbers and influence have continued to grow in the last two decades.

"In 2020, far-right extremists were responsible for 16 of 17 extremist killings in the U.S., according to the Anti-Defamation League, while in 2019, 41 of the 42 extremist killings were linked to the far right."

Look at us now. We can't protect our children from insane men with guns or from a damned pandemic. We can't even agree to pay to fill the potholes in our streets.

My city of ruins.

Twenty years later, I still mourn what happened. I mourn more for what it did to us.

We certainly had bigotry before that day. We had political discord and stupidity and selfishness. It just seems so much worse now. It's like bin Laden got what he wanted.

It doesn't have to be this way.

I mourn, but I've not lost hope. Gardens grow where our tears fall.

Working in the lab late one night

Oct 31, 2021

Knowledge is understanding that Frankenstein is not the monster. Wisdom is understanding that Frankenstein *is* the monster.

That statement, from source unknown, presented itself to me recently in a moment of serendipity just as I had decided to alter the way I celebrate Halloween. I'm so tired of hearing, "Aren't you a little too old to be trick-or-treating?"

So, taking the hint, this year I acquired a dusty copy of Mary Shelley's 19th-century Gothic novel, "Frankenstein," from the Central Library and also re-watched the classic 1931 movie version starring Boris Karloff. The novel is a little ponderous to Twitter-era sensibilities. The film is unintentionally funny. But despite their flaws, both are still enjoyable.

If the quote is confusing, it's probably because you're unfamiliar with the bones of the story, which have been diluted over the years to suit the purposes of advertising and satire.

In a nutshell: Frankenstein is a med-school dropout who raids graves and gallows to gruesomely acquire body parts, which he assembles into a person that he then brings to life. His creation — who is never actually given a name — escapes into an unsuspecting world after being treated cruelly by his creator. Largely innocent, but preternaturally strong and hideous in countenance, the creature raises the ire of pretty much everyone he meets until an ugly, out-of-control mob with pitchforks and torches, led by his creator, corners him and burns him to death.

So the "monster" isn't named Frankenstein — which not everybody knows. But it's Frankenstein who is truly monstrous — an understanding that requires just a little wisdom.

It's so easy to be mistaken when you don't know the full story — when, perhaps, one tiny part is pulled out, distorted and exaggerated.

"Frankenstein" isn't the only book I've read this month. After hearing the complaints from right-wing politicos about materials they dug up in school libraries and identified as "filth," I decided I'd better see what all the fuss was about. So, back to the library, I checked out the young readers' novels "Lawn Boy" by Jonathan Evison, "George" by Alex Gino and the graphic novel "Gender Queer" by Maia Kobabe — all about young people with gender issues who are trying to make their way in the world.

There were parts of each that made me a little uncomfortable *not* because they were especially explicit, but because I'm a heterosexual male of mature years, with all that entails. I can see where someone with limited worldly experience — knowledge rather than wisdom, let's say — might, on first instinct, be tempted to object.

But two facts tempered my judgment:

First of all, these books weren't written for me. Not every book is for every reader. I won't pretend to be the standard — that mine should be the final set of sensibilities on which all books are judged. (These days, I'm kind of glad that people are reading *anything*.)

Secondly, despite my occasional discomfort, there were also parts of all three books that I found to be relatable and rewarding.

The protagonist in each one struggles with self-doubts, fears and disapproval.

I've been there.

They also seek and find comfort, acceptance and success.

I've been there, too.

If a book can reassure LGBTQ kids that they're not monsters, but human, that they're worthy of love and have a place in the world, I think it belongs on the shelves. Too many are trying to convince them otherwise.

Some may agree with those principles and still think the stories could be told differently.

In my previous life as a librarian, I learned the difference between a selector and a censor. A selector looks for reasons to include a book in a collection, even if it's flawed: important information; a display of creative energy; a positive message.

A censor, on the other hand, looks for reasons to exclude a work: a bad word, an unpleasant scene, *any* reason to say no.

You'd think that people who are concerned about "cancel culture" would want to support selectors.

Instead . . . well.

I don't want to lean too far into the analogy of a mob with pitchforks and torches, chasing down what they don't understand. But it takes no special talent or courage to rile up an audience that already has a dim view of both LGBTQ people and public education.

It would take courage to say, *we should consider whether these books might have some value to their readers, even if we don't get it. And while we're at it, we should sit with some of these kids and listen to what they have to say.*

I had time for one more book this month: "GOP 2.0" by Lt. Gov. Geoff Duncan of Georgia. He's a Republican who is urging his party to abandon Trumpism and election lies. He presents a positive vision of a rewarding future for all Americans.

It's a little scary to me that courage is required to spread *that* message these days.

Happy Halloween. Save me some candy.

Watch the ripples change their size

Nov 17, 2021

After my dad said "Good night" and the lights went off, I huddled under the covers with — not a flashlight and a book, in my case, but a radio. At 14, I tuned in to that station in Chapel Hill with the soft-voiced DJ who played Bob Dylan and The Righteous Brothers. Or the Chicago station — amazing how far the airwaves travel — that played the "CBS Radio Mystery Theatre." This was my little hidden rebellious world. (Not that Dad would have minded *any* of that content earlier in the evening.) I traveled, by sound, to other places until they lulled me to sleep.

Kids. Powerful forces drive us toward whatever we think we need to ensure our survival and enrich our developing minds. Parents may fight it and they may prevail for some time. But human will wins out.

I think about that when I think about the current conservative rage to empty school library shelves of material they deem "inappropriate" — books that many didn't even know existed before their party began searching for another wedge to drive between the American people for political advantage.

So it is that outraged parents with heads full of conspiracy theories are accusing school boards and school librarians of everything just short of pedophilia because their library shelves — not their classes — contain titles that may be useful to a handful of confused and struggling children.

I have no doubt that the protesting parents are sincere. They're worried about their kids. That's perfectly understandable.

Many of them are also misguided and misinformed — especially if they think their kids might become gay or transgender because of a picture they saw in a graphic novel.

That's not how that works. That's not how *any* of that works.

But they continue to think so — to see a basic human biological factor as *sin*, as something they should punish as they would lying or shoplifting — despite the witness and life experience of literally millions of people throughout the world and history who say this is what they *are*, not what they *do*.

Admittedly, some school organizations are doing themselves no favors when they respond by asserting their expertise. They need to find ways to *pander* to parents' rights. Like their challengers.

But more important than the rights of parents are the rights of children.

In North Carolina, our constitution guarantees children the right to a sound, basic education.

They also have the right to live; the right to nourishment. And they deserve to be exposed to attitudes they might not find at home.

Children don't belong to their parents — parents belong to their children, as expediters and stewards and guides. They serve them poorly if they try to create younger versions of themselves.

We in the media try to avoid analogies that reference the unique horrors of the Holocaust and slavery. Anti-vaxxers who *choose* to wear yellow stars on their coats trivialize such atrocities.

But it's hard not to detect an atrocious stench coming from Spotsylvania County in Virginia, where two school board members last week advocated burning books about race and sexuality.

"I think we should throw those books in a fire," school board member Rabih Abuismail said. School board member Kirk Twigg said he wanted to "see the books before we burn them so we can identify within our community that we are eradicating this bad stuff."

Nazis burn books.

Americans don't.

They've been called on to resign and they should do so.

Even if they don't, though, even if this sanitizing witch hunt continues, they're going to lose.

According to comic-book news site CBR.com, following parental complaints of Jerry Craft's graphic novel "New Kid," the book's sales have increased. I suspect that's true of many of the books that conservatives like N.C. Lt. Gov. Mark Robinson have made controversial. Lots of kids are curious about the messages from which they're supposed to be shielded. They're going to read them.

You'd think parents would have learned by now. You'd think they'd remember their own childhoods.

Books are powerful; they open worlds and minds. The right books will teach oppressed kids that there's more to life than what they find in school or at home. They'll teach bullied kids that they can be different and still find a place in the world. They'll tell kids not to give up and not accept the present — things get better.

Some kids won't make it — they'll give in to the dark voices that say they're abominations who don't deserve to live.

But I have faith that most of them will make it. They have the resolve. They'll find the support. This is what David Bowie knew when he wrote:

These children that you spit on
As they try to change their world
Are immune to your consultations
They're quite aware of what they're going through.

Much more aware — and able to cope with reality — than the book burners.

Songs that voices never share

Dec 5, 2021

The Winston-Salem Journal has always opposed gerrymandering — even when Democrats did it.

I make the assertion in response to feedback I received after publishing our Nov. 18 editorial, "Ruthless by design," about the state Republican Party's efforts to fix the district maps to their unfair advantage.

How severe were the responses? Let's just say the word "hypocrite" was used more than once.

To some degree I'm not surprised. After all, hypocrisy is so rampant in politics these days that it's practically the norm. It's there in almost any partisan issue I could raise. I'm sure you're thinking of one or two right now.

But as far as the Journal's position on gerrymandering goes, I've got to reject the claim. Allow me to regale thee with the reasons why.

For one, the editorial in question notes that Democrats are trying to tip the scales, too, "in Illinois, Maryland, New York and Oregon," and that they're wrong to do so.

We also point out that "They did the same in North Carolina for decades when they controlled the legislature." In fact, every time these last few years that we've written about Republican gerrymandering, we've made a point of saying, "the Democrats did it and it was wrong then, too." Nobody here is trying to give Democrats a pass.

In fact, even when the Democrats were in charge of the legislature, we condemned the practice.

For instance, in 2002, we wrote: "The Democratic redistricting plan of 2001 was something just short of politically pornographic. Democrats in control . . . wove districts through the state's counties and towns with one goal in mind: preserving the Democratic majority in both houses. . . . Republicans were right to sue to overturn the plans."

In 2005, we wrote: "The ruling party — in North Carolina, the Democrats — jams as many of the minority party into minority 'ghetto' districts as possible, thus assuring the election of the minority party there. With these voters out of the way, legislators can then configure the remaining districts in ways that keep the majority party in power.

"The result has been a disaster for the American political system."

Even in 2013, after Republicans took over, we let Democrats have it: "The redistricting process is a travesty. For more than a century, the Democratic Party maintained a tighter grip on state politics than it deserved simply by gerrymandering legislative and congressional districts."

That's the *opposite* of hypocrisy. That's consistency.

I understand that some might find that concept . . . foreign. Confusing.

All along the way, we've also called for an independent redistricting commission.

So did Republican Senate leader Phil Berger, when his party was locked in the minority.

His position has changed now.

But as proud as I am of the Journal's consistency, I can't really take credit for it. I've only been the editorial page editor for the last three and a half years. It's one of my predecessors at this desk who decided that gerrymandering was wrong, no matter who did it.

The truth is that most of our editorials are based on longstanding principles. The Journal has historically supported policies that favor local business initiatives; a strong educational system; responsible environmental stewardship; the value of the arts; and morality and accountability from our elected leaders. In a literal sense, our editorial policies are *conservative*. They don't shift according to which party is in power.

Despite my defense, I know that some readers will still feel sour about our condemnation of the Republican project. One or two I hear from regularly wouldn't be happy unless the entire editorial excoriated the Democrats. But if we added a sentence in parentheses — (The Republicans are doing it, too) — that would be enough to send them into a tizzy.

That's what happens when party comes before principle.

But even though we try to be fair, we've also got to be honest. Yes, the Democrats once put their thumb on the scale. But that thumb was light enough that in 2010, voters were able to relieve them of their majority.

The Republicans learned from their mistake and are *right now* trying to implement district maps that will keep them in power permanently, even if their numbers dwindle, even if a majority of voters want them out.

As a practical matter, which attempt to manipulate elections should concern us more — the one from 20 years ago or the one occurring now?

Bold actions sometimes have unforeseen consequences. Even the most partisan Republicans should hope these gerrymandered maps are tossed out by the courts. North Carolinians deserve the opportunity to select their representatives — not the other way around.

Where the sand's turning to gold

Dec 31, 2021

In 2021, we lost Michael Nesmith.

It was a couple of weeks ago that the 78-year-old Texas singer/songwriter/actor passed on to the great circle sky. Known widely to the public as one fourth of the Pre-Fab Four, The Monkees — Weren't they good? They made me happy — and to aging hipsters like me as a country-rock prophet and a media innovator, equal parts silliness and rumbling thunder, his death just left me feeling sad, left me nine times blue. It became a focal point, the symbol of other losses this year, personal and public. It seemed the final insulting act of a year that repeatedly spit on us.

In 2021, I lost Red. One of the wild foxes I visit on a regular basis, in a field on the south side of town that I call Fox-a-Lago, she vanished at the same time that a dead fox was found in Washington Park. That fox didn't look like Red to me — Red's brow seemed less furrowed, her lovely snout longer — but it's hard to believe the timing was a coincidence.

Her daughter, Blondie, disappeared for a few days, as if in mourning.

The mood was both tempered and taunted by the best book I read this year, "Fox 8" (of course there's a fox in the title, and foxes in the story), by short-story master George Saunders. It shares the theme of disenchantment that I think was thrust on many of us, who expected reason and civilization to be a more effective deterrent to disease. I recommend it for everyone — the library has a copy — not only for the foxes, but for the questions it raises about human behavior — questions that deserve answers.

I don't want to spoil it, so that's all I'll say.

As the year stumbles and grumbles to its end, I feel somber. Many downtown storefronts are closed and dusty. The mound of dirt in what's supposed to be Merschel Plaza has sprouted a lawn. This week's pleasant, unseasonable temperatures have been accompanied by dark and dreary skies. Many times this year I felt sadness swell inside my chest as I witnessed unthinking anger and resurging prejudice.

But the entire year wasn't grim, of course. There were episodes of joy and humor and comfort.

One that made me laugh out loud came from a tweet posted on Dec. 8 by a clinician who calls himself Adam "Ghost of Christmas meh":

> *Had a 6 y/o come in to the 5-11 vaccine clinic, tear his shirt off, sit down, look at the RN, and say "do it." Pretty bad ass, we were all afraid of him after that.*

If only that kid's courage could be shared. Maybe in a vaccine or something.

A friend of a friend told me about setting up the Christmas tree this year. For the past 10 years, along with the ornaments and lights, she's pulled from a box a note her husband wrote before dying of cancer — instructions for setting up the tree. It's become an annual reminder of the meticulous care he had for all things, including her.

Tomorrow I'll put on the coffee, then go on my traditional First of January hike. The Earth will turn, the moon will wax and wane. Wildflowers will grow in my backyard.

When Blondie returned to Fox-a-Lago, she walked toward me more boldly, as if to say, *this is my yard now.* She's been joined by a larger, darker-furred stranger. In a couple of months, there could be new kits tumbling over each other, happy to be part of the world.

In the song "Me & Magdalena," which Benjamin Gibbard wrote for Nesmith to sing on the final Monkees album in 2016, he included the lines:

> *But know everything lost will be recovered*
> *When you drift into the arms of the undiscovered*

I don't know if that's a universal law, but it makes me feel better.

For all the loss, for all the suffering, the arms of the undiscovered wait to carry us into an unwritten future. Nobody knows what will happen next.

I fervently hope that the new year will bring new entrepreneurs to these streets and storefronts. I hope that new music will echo through the buildings' canyons and new underground artists will invade and scandalize the City of Arts and Innovation, leaving the staid norms clutching their pearls. I hope the foxes will continue to run wild, safe from our grasp.

See you in 2022.

Where the world cannot find me

Jan 23, 2022

That snow last week was just what I needed.

I rose early Sunday morning, as I do, while the ground was still bare. But I didn't have long to wait before the snow began to fall, steadily, in earnest, collecting quickly in yards and on the road, covering both like a fluffy coat of flour. I watched it fall from the comfort and warmth of my workroom, cup of coffee in hand and WFDD in the background.

I thought about "Wallace the Brave," who would have spent such a day searching for Bigfoot tracks.

Me, I just sat there slurping.

And that describes much of the day. I'd already run all the necessary errands. The power never wavered. There was absolutely nothing on my schedule except to follow my whims, which left me watching the snow accumulate.

Eventually the coffee was gone, and I moved to my reading chair, where I finished "Nature's Best Hope" by Douglas W. Tallamy, an ecology professor who urges his readers to stop mowing their lawns — at least parts of their lawns — and plant webs of native species that would better support wildlife and better support us. His book, recommended by a friend — I got my copy at the Central Library — is eminently readable and enlightening. To someone like me, who never had a lawn until a year ago and still doesn't know what to do with it, the idea is an easy sell. I imagine, in the spring, planting oak and black cherry trees, milkweed for the monarchs and fireweed and woodland phlox for the color, then letting them go.

I also dream of digging a fox den in the backyard, but that's out of reach. For now.

Speaking of foxes, the ones I know had a snow day as well.

At the beginning of the year, a fellow fox lover and I invested in a couple of trail cams, which we set up in Fox-a-Lago — the field not far from me where a leash of wild foxes lives — to see what we could see. We've harvested hundreds of 10-second video clips featuring Blondie and her new companion, Scruffy Milton, as well as other foxes, both red and gray. We've also watched the escapades of raccoons, deer, crows and other birds that I'd need the assistance of Ron Morris to identify, as they jockey with each other for sniffing rights.

There are the crows, pecking at the peanuts that I left the night before. They look so crafty, and seem to communicate effectively with each other via shrugs.

There's Scruffy being chased away from the field by a bulky raccoon — then, mustering his courage, chasing the raccoon away.

There's Scruffy and Blondie dancing, so it seems, front paws on each other's shoulders.

Then the snow fell. Blondie continued hunting through the storm, impervious to the wind and wetness. After it stopped, Scruffy dug and found something tasty that kept him busy for more than an hour. Later, he stood in the field staring into the distance, the wind ruffling his coat, thinking fox thoughts. In the daytime, against a stark, snow-covered background, the foxes' red fur popped with vibrancy.

This natural world, of grass and snow, crows and insects — it's different from the one we've constructed. There's an honesty to it, a simple presence. I wouldn't want to live without central air and indoor plumbing, but I fear we miss out on something essential when we separate ourselves from nature and live virtually instead.

My snow day ended with some hot chocolate and a deep, restful sleep.

After the long weekend, it was back to the office, where misinformation had been piling up in my inbox. Yes, some of former President Trump's lawsuits over the election were dismissed for standing — which is a legitimate legal standard — but many were dismissed for their lack of legitimate merit. No, 75% of COVID-19 deaths are not related to comorbidities — CDC director Rochelle Walensky's statement has been distorted. Of course there's no legislation that says, "African Americans aren't allowed to vote," that would be too obvious; instead, some state legislatures are making voting more difficult for people who live in Black-majority areas by reducing polling sites, among other tactics.

Google is free.

More winter weather is expected this weekend, but I doubt it'll be severe enough to quiet the city, like last weekend. I'll still sit at my window with my coffee, thinking about the foxes, able to withstand the blustering wind and snow without even flinching. Their coats kept them warm.

Their presence, their existence, keeps me warm.

Dreams walking in broad daylight

Feb 20, 2022

Here's how the conversation began:

"Your articles on the (fertilizer plant) fire have avoided giving credit to the exceptional fire management of the Winston-Salem fire department," she wrote. "They deserve credit for prompt response by getting the gas company to turn off gas to the plant, the concern for safety of fire fighters, and the safety of all in the surrounding area. . . . Can you just once say that we were blessed to have prevented what could have been a much worse disaster and give credit to Chief Trey Mayo and the Winston-Salem's firefighters?"

For the record, I agree with that assessment of our firefighters. And I feel safe in saying that our reporters and editors in the news department agree, also.

For that matter, I can't help but feel like their valor came through in the news stories — that's likely how this reader, and others, recognized it.

But — well, as I replied:

"Thanks for writing. You're entitled to your opinion, and I don't want to be argumentative, but I'd have to disagree with you.

"First of all, it's not the purpose of a news story to give credit or place blame, but to report what's happening. A news

146

story that was purposely effusive about the fire department would exceed its bounds (and, I'll add here, might look a bit unprofessional).

"My section of the paper, though, the Opinion page, *can* give credit and did so on Feb. 3. You may have missed it."

And I provided a link to our editorial, which, among other things, referred to "our safety professionals — police and firefighters — who step forward with courage and dedication, putting their own well-being on the line for our benefit."

The reader was kind enough to reply:

"In order to enjoy the rest of your paper, I have to avoid reading the Editorial Section completely. There is so much liberal biases in your editorials I cannot stomach or bother to try to find something positive."

So. Not to pick on my friend, but I feel just a little frustrated that she complained that we didn't do the thing we actually did and she didn't know we did it because she refuses to read the section of the paper where we do that sort of thing.

I also think some would disagree that supporting our firefighters is the result of a "liberal bias."

Something's missing in that picture — and it's not our praise for firefighters.

I could go in several different directions here. But the point I'm really trying to make is this: The news department isn't supposed to be for or against even a stalwart outfit like our own fire department or a hero like Fire Chief Trey Mayo. A news story is just supposed to tell you what happened.

A good reporter will provide context, yes — and, with hope, write with the kind of skill that will make you want to read the story.

But reporters aren't advocates.

That's my job.

I've noted before that we in the news industry don't always do a good job of explaining our various roles and objectives. There's just not a baked-in mechanism for it.

But I don't think it's that lack alone that leaves some readers confused or dissatisfied. After careful analysis and observation, I have to at least consider this possibility: that some readers *want* their news to be biased — they just want it to be biased their way.

Maybe that's the expectation that evolves from consuming too much cable TV and social media.

But that's not the way news should operate.

A day or two after the above exchange, the Journal printed the story "Fire investigators begin work: City OKs resolution thanking firefighters."

On the same front page, we had a story about a volunteer fire chief who has been accused of improprieties.

Do either of those stories represent the Journal's position on the value of firefighters?

Of course not. Those stories are intended to tell you what's happening in the community, good or bad. So you'll know.

That's what an unbiased news department is supposed to do. I don't think anyone in the area does it better.

Whether the public wants that . . . is up to the public.

I realize it's bad form to criticize what may be my own readers — but I think you're generally a knowledgeable bunch. And you look good, too.

From Russia with love

Mar 6, 2022

Despite the vast array of speakers at the circus-like Conservative Political Action Conference in Orlando last weekend, it's Lauren Witzke, the 2020 Republican candidate for the Senate from Delaware, who may win the weekend's badge for distasteful and embarrassing takes. Speaking on the Feb. 24 CrossTalk (whatever that is), she had nothing but praise for Russian President Vladimir Putin's invasion of Ukraine. Where many might call his nation a dictatorial oligarchy in practice, Witzke's take was different:

"Russia is a Christian nationalist nation," she said. "I actually support Putin's right to protect his people and always put his people first, but also protect their Christian values."

She continued: "I identify more with Putin's Christian values than I do with Joe Biden."

That's the Joe Biden who is the U.S. president, a life-long Catholic who attends church and prays regularly.

And that's the Putin whose artillery is currently targeting schools and hospitals in Ukraine.

Incidentally, Witzke also believes that cannibalistic pedophiles are secretly controlling the world order and that former President Trump was sent by God to expose them, in between rounds of golf and lying about the 2020 election.

But she's not alone in her affection for Russia. Even though many conservatives who previously praised Putin are now backpedaling as his rogue nation invades Ukraine, it's undeniable that many of them have been flirting with the Russian president, whose "Christian values" include poisoning and murdering his political opponents, for quite some time. I wonder how close that allegiance is to the growing Republican disdain for democracy, as exemplified in statements from Utah Sen. Mike Lee — from whom I first heard democracy described as "mob rule" — and conservative commentator and author Mark Levin, who used similar anti-democracy language while he addressed CPAC last weekend.

I'm sure many are wondering how it came to this: That some staunch patriots on the right have come to enthusiastically support the leader of a geo-political adversary, a worldwide sponsor of terrorism, a corrupt billionaire who learned his politics from the KGB, who is now aggressively attacking a foreign nation that did nothing wrong. How did this happen?

Several signposts stand out, but one in particular keeps recurring to me. I think that many on the right, especially conservative Christians, now support Russia over the U.S. because of their fixation on and opposition toward gay people.

If it please the court:

The legalization of same-sex marriage in 2015 was a bitter pill for many conservatives to swallow, including Ralph Reed, the founder of the Faith & Freedom Coalition. I remember seeing him on NBC's Meet the Press, his eyes dark as if he'd been crying for days, arguing, in essence, that if he and his allies weren't allowed to discriminate against gay people, these same gay people would be allowed to call Reed and his allies "bigots."

Not exactly a "do unto others" moment.

After the court decision, evangelical leaders began flocking to Russia — a country that holds a hard line against homosexuality — to meet Putin. Among them was Franklin Graham, who had a warm meeting with Putin in 2015 in which Putin reportedly talked about his mother's Christian faith.

Although being gay isn't illegal in Russia, and homosexuality was declassified as a mental illness there in 1999, bullying, death threats and physical attacks are a regular feature of life for gay people in Russia.

In 2013, Putin signed into law a bill banning the "propaganda of nontraditional sexual relations to minors," a law that was widely condemned by human rights groups like Amnesty International and Human Rights Watch for being overly broad and vague. It reportedly led to an increase in violence against gay people.

It's the same sort of law that was once used to imprison and torture American missionaries.

Talking with his new "dictatorship-curious" evangelical fans, Putin touted the superiority of his "Christian nation" view to Western values, which evangelicals saw as increasingly corrupt and overly permissive.

That message resonated with them. It fit their frustration at not being able to maintain a nation in their own image.

Some conservative Christians have long had a great deal of difficulty accepting that they live in a pluralistic society in which they're not allowed to be the sole arbiters of legal, educational and cultural decisions. They never learned that most primary of lesson: to share.

They have rights, of course. They can condemn homosexuality if they so choose. They can preach against it every Sunday, they can teach it to their children, they can broadcast it on TV, radio and Twitter (though none of those outlets are required to accommodate them). I disagree wholeheartedly, but I support their right to free speech — the right their idol, Putin, denies his own people. Liberty means letting people do things you don't want them to do.

But every other American, regardless of race, gender or religion, just as convinced of the validity of their religious and political views, has the same right to speak in support of dignity and equality for gay people. *The same right.*

Liberty means letting people do things you don't want them to do.

This nation is not the sole property of conservative Christians. They can't have it.

There are other reasons why conservative Christians might side with Russia. I believe this one, though, their unending desire to push back on equal rights for gay people, to be the most indefensible and hypocritical. Here's why:

In the Bible, Jesus said that divorce, unless the result of adultery, was a sin. But we never hear about Christian bakers quizzing their clients over whether they need the cake for their first or second (or third) wedding. The Bible condemns drunkenness. But we never read about Christian venue owners asking their clients if they plan to serve alcohol. It's only over homosexuality that they'll risk their livelihoods. They've selected gay people to be the particular targets of their ire.

Conservative Christians rub elbows every day with liars, gluttons, the greedy, hoarders of wealth, the vain and proud, adulterers, and they readily adapt — it's only gay people that they so fervently desire to punish.

Their antipathy has led them to be willing to sacrifice the lives of LGBTQ youth. They vote for politicians like Texas Gov. Greg Abbott, who write laws that place vulnerable children in the path of harm, that threaten to rip them from their parents, that will lead to an increase in bullying, depression, anxiety and suicide.

And in their pursuit of the right to persecute, they now embrace *an opponent of their own country* — a liar, a killer, a destroyer of the homes of children.

That's a far greater sin than loving the wrong person.

Of course, *#notallofus*. I know that not all conservative Christians think that Putin deserves their backing or that gay people deserve their punishment. Same-sex marriage became the law of the land with the support of several Republican legislators after their children asked, "Dad, don't you want me to get married someday?"

Some in the evangelical community let their light shine by supporting immigrants in need without requiring religious conversion. Some have long-standing relations with Ukraine and support its people now. Some have hearts more attuned to kindness and justice than the power to control others' lives. They despair over the authoritarian direction their colleagues have taken. They revolt against the anti-American strain of conservative Christianity that now uses the tools of fear and deceit in an attempt to turn our nation into something more closely aligned with Russia.

Biden is right when he says that we're in a fight for the soul of our nation. There seems to be a similar battle taking place in the Southern Baptist Convention, as well as other large

Christian organizations that have suffered scandals over ethical concerns.

Putin and other autocratic leaders are fighting to eliminate democracy throughout the world, and rule instead by intimidation and corruption. It's shameful to see that they have allies in the U.S.

On which side should *any* of us ultimately align — the side of oppression or the side of freedom? The side of cruelty or the side of compassion?

No nation, no political party or religious body can make the decision for us. Each of us has to decide for ourselves. And act accordingly.

Find the cost of freedom

Mar 13, 2022

God told her she would win.

"I have conquered it already. It is mine. I am claiming the victory."

That's what Bianca Gracia, a pro-Trump Republican, said a week after filing for the Texas state Senate, District 11, earlier this year.

"If you do not show up, then you will be held accountable, because I have been appointed and assigned for this position, and God is testing you all," she warned a group of local pastors.

But despite the endorsement of the Almighty, she received only 7.5% of the vote, losing to the candidate who received 62.6%, The (Texas) Independent reported last week.

Of course, she didn't really lose. Not legitimately. She now believes that local Republicans cheated her — cheated *God* — out of her victory. Which is something you'd think God could prevent. Being God.

This is kind of a rare story, but it isn't unique; from time to time, candidates believe they hear God's voice whispering in their ear, only to later realize it was the wind.

Sometimes, the candidate who claims God's favor does win.

I've never found a reliable method, though, to discern between legitimate claims of God's endorsement and illegitimate.

Is it a matter of winning? That proves God's favor?

Some observers would choke before admitting God's selection of President Joe Biden or House Speaker Nancy Pelosi.

I thought about this while continuing to ponder the topic I wrote about last week: the allegiance that some conservative Christians have come to express for Russia and Russian President Vladimir Putin over their own nation and president, even as Russia murderously pillages Ukraine. As I wrote, I believe it springs from many channels, especially their bitter disappointment that gay people have increasingly been awarded equality in American society.

But beyond that, it occurs to me that it's probably true that Russia, with Putin's claim to lead a "Christian nation," checks more boxes for them than a country that is built on principles of equality, freedom and democracy.

When you think about it, despite all the insistent rhetoric about ours being "a Christian nation," the ties between Christianity and the United States are tenuous, more an accidental, rarely examined synthesis of competing loyalties than anything. There's no democracy in the Bible — none at all. There's no Bill of Rights. There's no freedom of religion or freedom of speech. Essentially there's belief and obedience or eternal punishment. So says the fundamentalist view.

And there's no Bible or Jesus in the U.S. Constitution, or in the Federalist Papers that explain the Constitution's reasoning. Most of the Ten Commandments are constitutionally unenforceable.

In the Old Testament, God's prophets anointed kings, who then sat on the throne with access to the nation's wealth — not to mention thousands of concubines — and ruled by dictate.

I can't help wondering if that standard played a role in how the evangelical community was so willing to overlook former President Trump's vast moral defects, as best exemplified by his serial adultery. The king does as the king pleases.

In the New Testament, though not exactly a governing body, Judas' replacement in the apostolic ranks was chosen by lottery. Paul appointed himself to that august board by force of his own will.

Voting for those offices would be tantamount to overriding God's will.

I think some conservative Christians have come to realize that America is not set up to favor them indefinitely — not when others have the same rights and privileges. It just took them a little while to get there.

And that's where I find author Mark Levin, an intelligent man and a compelling speaker, who at CPAC two weeks ago condemned populism and nationalism along with democracy, claiming that constitutional principles should take precedent over "mob rule."

There's some merit to what he says, but I have to break with him, and other Republicans, when they claim that our rights come not from the Constitution per se, but that they're "God-given."

That's problematic for several reasons, among them that the authors of the Constitution never claimed to be speaking for God.

But what frightens me the most about the claim is that if conservative Christians were allowed to enumerate those rights — and who else would they allow to define them? — they would just happen to coincide with the rights conservatives like. The constitutional principles of freedom and equality, especially for gay people and minorities, would suffer (not to mention freedom of the press).

Their insistence on the right to carry personal arsenals and deploy them aggressively would be even more stringently enforced, despite the lack of AR-15s in the Bible and the biblical injunction, "if a man strikes you on one cheek, turn to him the other, also."

Whatever your denomination, if you think the Bible provides the government with a mandate to force children to bow their heads in prayer, but not to feed the poor, you're doing it wrong.

But since their theocratic vision meets so much resistance in the civilized West, they look to the East and see Putin; ruthless, confident and in harmony with their God's heavy hand.

Or, as Stuart Stevens, a former Republican political operative, put it in a recent tweet, "They see him as a white Christian nationalist strongman against the corruption of modern society. In Putin's Russia there are no gays, no women in power, corrupted wealth is just reward for ruling class and no dissent is allowed. It's exactly the world Trump & many in @GOP want."

It's a country, incidentally, with no separation of church and state. The Russian Orthodox Church has supported Putin's invasion of Ukraine, with Patriarch Kirill, its leader, referring to the conflict as a "metaphysical" struggle against a godless international order, as a struggle to keep liberal foreigners from holding "gay parades" in Moscow.

Or, as we call it, democracy.

Incidentally, Russia has the highest abortion rate in the world.

I realize that many conservative Christians think they would prefer living in a theocracy. In fact, that's the problem in a nutshell.

They should be careful for what they wish. History is replete with biblical arbiters who have, in the name of their various sects, treated their fellow believers harshly. Torturously, even.

But as the demographics continue to shift against them, I believe we can expect more attempts to suppress voting, more censorship of oppositional ideas and more complaints about democracy, still couched in terms of returning America to its Christian heritage as they attempt to bend the system to meet their theocratic desires. Until suddenly it will stop.

Some fear that if Republicans regain Congress and the presidency, we'll never have another free election. They'll change the law, Russian-style, to stay in power.

I might think that was hyperbole except for the degree to which they're already bad-mouthing democracy and justifying gerrymandering — and except for their promotion of the Big Lie that Democrats habitually win elections by cheating. They insist this is true, despite their inability to prove, in one single court case, that widespread cheating has occurred — and despite the fact that *not one single audit or recount* has changed the result of a state's tally.

It's become a literal article of faith for many Republicans, who need no evidence — they just need God's voice whispering in their ear.

But it doesn't have to be like that. Despite their dissatisfaction, I think conservative Christians should still see the U.S. as a welcoming home worthy of loyalty and patriotism. They should embrace democracy as the best of all the flawed political systems — especially when compared to Russia's — and even when they lose.

In the Gospel of Mark, when the Pharisees approached Jesus with a "gotcha" question about taxes, he replied, "Render unto Caesar what is Caesar's and unto God what is God's."

Jesus presented these as two separate realms. Despite the desire of some for him to rise up and throw off the yoke of the Roman oppressor and rebuild Israel's glory, he had other things in mind. He spoke of a kingdom that had no ties to nation or party; one that transcended those human constructs.

Don't take my word for it. Read the Gospels.

In America, the adherents of his way are free to worship and speak as they please, just like everyone else. They can share in the nation's bounty, just like everyone else. They just can't *rule*.

Why isn't that enough?

Open up your morning light

Apr 3, 2022

They're called forsythia, these bright yellow blossoms that have appeared recently at Fox-a-Lago, the field near Washington Park where a friend and I regularly watch wild red foxes play. They're complemented by violets scattered across the ground.

Other colorful buds are sprouting in my neighborhood, from Japanese cherry trees and red buds — white, pink, purple blooms. The bluebirds and sparrows round out the color wheel.

Back toward the end of January, we saw that a couple of our foxes (not "our," but, you know) had developed mange, a malady that often leads to death. A little research led us to Wildlife Rehab Inc., which taught us how to treat them by putting ivermectin in food for them.

Yep, that ivermectin. My friend had to explain to the farm store clerk, "No, it's not for me."

Such is life in 2022.

Two months later, we'll soon need a new name for the one we've been calling "Skinny Tail." The fur on his brush, like everywhere else, is getting thicker.

A few days ago Blondie, the boldest of the foxes, sat relaxed on the ground not far from where I sat, she thinking her fox thoughts, me wondering what those thoughts were.

The phrase "culture of life" popped into my head. I felt — and maybe Blondie did, too — an appreciation for irrepressible life, which thrives when given the chance.

Life is the birthright of an entire planet (and maybe more). As the flowers and foxes attest, it's full of richness and variety. It's usually intertwined with other life.

The phrase "culture of life" crosses my desk at work from time to time, usually when either abortion or euthanasia are in the news. These extremes — conception and death — unfortunately seem to be the only aspects of such a culture that some ever promote or defend.

Surely a society that truly valued life would honor and protect *all* of it. It would work to reduce agents that are harmful to life and promote those that help it flourish and prosper.

The news today is full of harmful legislation being passed that makes life more difficult for transgender children, whose lives are already hard. Some 56% of trans youth attempt suicide before age 18, according to the American Academy of Pediatrics.

That rate drops about 73% when they're allowed to live as they decide they should.

Social scientists Tey Meadow and Kristina R. Olson, writing in this month's Scientific American, say, "Social acceptance and affirmative support are the keys to mental health for transgender children."

These kids struggle — not because they're "confused about which bathroom to use," as some say in an attempt to trivialize their agency. They struggle against bullies and ignorance and arrogant religiosity, sometimes from within their own families.

And these new laws and policies being pushed by Republicans "propose the very opposite: encouraging the mistreatment of trans youth and inciting fear in compassionate adults," Meadow and Olson say.

Robert Foster, a Mississippi Republican, recently said he wants supporters of transgender rights "to be lined up against (a) wall before a firing squad to be sent to an early judgment."

He's talking about parents who are trying to keep their children alive.

In Texas, officials have pretty much declared war on all gay people, most recently by removing suicide prevention resources for LGBTQ kids from government websites. Republican legislators across the country are pulling out all the stops to deny kids resources — books, the counsel of understanding adults, access to medical care — that may keep them alive.

None of that contributes to a culture of life.

Utah Gov. Spencer Cox, a Republican and a Mormon, understands this.

"When in doubt . . . I always try to err on the side of kindness, mercy and compassion," he wrote recently while vetoing a cruel measure put forward by his state's legislature. "I don't understand what they are going through or why they feel the way they do. But I want them to live."

That's how you promote a culture of life.

Unfortunately, his pleas fell on deaf ears. His legislature overrode the veto.

This one issue is just the tip of a rapidly melting iceberg. We stand today with the power to make ourselves extinct, through a culture of permissive greed, indifference to environmental collapse and tolerance for human suffering.

A true culture of life would work to prevent that.

If we do destroy ourselves, that won't be the end. The planet, with its bacteria and moss, its wolves and ravens, will live on. Without us.

Thunder and lightning
couldn't be bolder

May 8, 2022

So I got COVID.

It knocked me off my feet for a few days, then I was shaky on them for a few more.

But at this point, with negative test results and my strength returning, I'm eager to get back to living. Like so many others in the same boat, *I made it*, thanks to support from friends and vaccines.

One friend tells me of another who chose not to be vaccinated, saying, "God will protect me."

Some who expected such protection have been disappointed, as have their survivors. Maybe God is, as Ian Anderson once wrote, "a lover of life but a player of pawns." My friend's friend is still healthy — that's all that matters. To him.

Last week while on a Gatorade binge, I remembered an old joke, so old that you'll probably reach the punchline before me:

A man dies and is greeted at the pearly gates by St. Peter, who proceeds to show him around.

"See this golden street? It leads to the Big Guy's throne. And over there is the shop where, when we're done, you can go get your wings. To your left you'll see the 24-hour omelet station."

"What's that over there?" the man asks, indicating a little wooden chapel in the distance. Singing emanates from it.

"Shh," Peter says. "That's the Baptists and they think they're the only ones here."

Back in the day, I was as likely to hear the joke *from* the good-natured Baptists as *about* them. Other versions tease members of other denominations.

Today, it reminds me that there are those among the faithful who do think, where they stand now, that they're the only ones here — or the only ones who matter, anyway.

This came to me before we learned how close they are to making their mark on our nation's abortion laws. It came, actually, as I considered the restrictions some are trying to impose on our schools and public libraries — and their complaints about those who don't fit their mold.

Despite the "obscenity" and "pornography" rhetoric, not to mention "critical race theory," the bulk of the books they want removed seem to be by gay or Black authors — and seem, on examination, to contain none of those elements. They include biographies of former first lady Michelle Obama and author Toni Morrison, as well as "In the Night Kitchen," by Maurice Sendak; "They Called Themselves K.K.K.: The Birth of an American Terrorist Group," by Susan Campbell Bartoletti; and even the sticky-sweet board book "Everywhere Babies," by Susan Meyers, which tacitly depicts what some would interpret to be, but don't *have* to be, same-sex couples.

Those who object apparently think they're the only ones here.

In January, Ridgeland, Miss., Mayor Gene McGee withheld $110,000 from his city's library system, claiming that, as a Christian, *he* couldn't support the library — a public accommodation that serves *everyone* — while it circulated "homosexual material."

He thinks he's the only one here.

Also in January, Jeremy Glenn, the superintendent of Granbury Independent School District in North Texas, ordered a group of school librarians to remove books about LGBTQ topics, telling them, "Here in this community, we're going to be conservative." He also told them that if their political beliefs differed from the majority, "You better hide it."

They think they're the only ones here.

In March, Randy Bishop, a right-wing Michigan radio host who's running for public office, complained about TV commercials featuring interracial couples: "Can't even watch a college basketball tournament without commercials telling me I have to feel guilty because I think a family should be a white mom, a white dad and white kids."

I very much doubt that any commercial meant to sell a product is an attempt to make anyone feel guilty — except for not buying the product. But for Bishop and others of his ilk, the important thing about the very *existence* of a mixed-race family, on TV or in real life, is its effect on white people.

They think they're the only ones here.

You may say those are fringe voices, and I wish they were, but what was on the far reaches of the conservative frontier five years ago — like QAnon and the "great replacement" theory shouted by neo-Nazis marching through Charlottesville — is running for office today. I could fill this page with such incidents.

I try to be generous, but the word that keeps coming back to me is *arrogance*.

There has to be a more graceful way to deal with people whose beliefs and backgrounds differ than trying to bury them.

Other parents want their children to know that gay kids exist and shouldn't be bullied or belittled.

They want their children to know that there is racism in our nation's history; it's real and it's wrong.

They want their children to be aware that there are other people in the world.

Thanks to the hatred they face, they're under no illusion that they're the only ones here.

A bright spot in the nighttime

May 22, 2022

How I wanted to see
the rising moon turn red.
But it was not to be,
so I went to sleep instead.

A week ago I was preparing to watch the full moon shift behind the shadow of the Earth, thus turning blood-red — a rare and dramatic event that would occur more or less around midnight, and last for about 85 minutes.

Unfortunately, it quickly became apparent that there would be nothing to see. A high and wide blanket of clouds, dark gray, coated the sky. The forecast called for the same all night long.

The NASA telescope feed I'd expected to be my Plan B didn't work out, either; it also seemed to be trapped under clouds.

I still have distinct memories of past blood-moon eclipses, eerie and enigmatic. Sometimes a memory is enough.

So I turned in.

The next morning I tended to the small garden I've planted, at the urging of friends who think I don't have enough to do. I'm growing sunflowers, strawberries and weeds. It's a new development for me and I don't know what to expect. But the strawberries, those that turn red, taste sweet.

At Fox-a-Lago, the field near Washington Park where a skulk of wild red foxes hang out, Scalawag and Blondie seem to be thriving.

My fox-loving friend and I once called Scalawag "Skinny Tail," but after our treatment relieved his mange, that had to change. He now sports a fluffy brush and a pretty face suitable for the cover of GQ. He's energetic, tromping around on giant paws that make him seem part horse.

We assume that Blondie's a mom, because the season is right and her shape recently morphed from full-bodied to svelte. Her coat is now a bit ragged, as we'd expect from a harried vixen with kits demanding food and attention. A neighbor thinks she spied a couple of small foxes playing in the field late one night, but Blondie has yet to introduce them to us or to the trail cams that catch plenty of raccoons and possums. We just don't know what to think, so we'll keep watching.

One evening as we sat waiting to see our friends, the wind blew vigorously, shaking the leaves on the 90-foot-tall trees like tambourines, swaying their limbs like dancers. It continued for some time, a combination symphony and ballet. The owls and crows added a choral component.

It was the best show in town.

Then Blondie came out and sat on the hill near us. She looked a little shy and sad and we imagined that she just wanted some company, even the company of big furless things who don't speak fox.

Just to sit and think, or to sit and not think, is a luxury for us, but I imagine it's a regular feature of fox life.

Of the many nutty things Elon Musk has said in recent times — I'm convinced he's trolling us all, tickled that people take him seriously — his comparison of China, which has "a lot of super-talented, hard-working people," to the U.S., where "people are trying to avoid going to work at all," may be the nuttiest.

I mean, he says that like it's a bad thing. I'm all for putting in a good day's work, but if America has any overarching work-related problem, "great resignation" notwithstanding, it's working ourselves to early graves, and for lower pay and fewer benefits than many of our counterparts in European countries receive.

As some wise guy once noted, "Nobody ever lies in his death bed and says, 'I should have spent more time at the office.'"

Me, I need more time sitting in this field. More time counting the peaches on the peach tree. More time trying to figure out how Joan Didion can write one thing and make you understand that she means something else entirely. More time taste-testing pancakes and coffee in roadside diners. More time rummaging through yard sales. More time doodling running foxes. More time watching the moon.

There's work to be done. There are serious issues to deal with today. We've got to face them.

But we miss out on something when we fail to make time for the real world.

A couple of weeks ago, one of the provocateurs I monitor on Twitter, former Illinois Rep. Joe Walsh, tweeted, "Spent all morning on Twitter. When I put my phone down, I was convinced Civil War was coming to America tomorrow. Spent all afternoon out walking & talking. The park, the Zoo, farmers markets, a coffee shop. When I got home, I was convinced next week would be just another week."

I hear ya, Joe. I hear ya, from the hill where I sit, watching the foxes play, listening to the wind symphony.

A million dead-end streets

Jun 19, 2022

Brace yourself. This is going to be dark.

Former pastor Todd Turner Brock of a High Point church pleaded guilty to charges of solicitation to commit first-degree sexual exploitation of a minor, participating in the prostitution of a 17-year-old boy and dissemination of obscenity in 2007.

Former deacon Guy Ellis Carr Jr., also of a High Point church, was convicted of eight counts of indecent liberties with a minor in 2009.

Brian "Doug" Goodrich Jr., then an intern in a Raleigh church, was sentenced to 13 years in prison in 2007 after pleading guilty on two counts of statutory sex offense, four counts of first-degree sexual exploitation of a minor and two counts of taking indecent liberties with a child.

These are just a few of the 40 North Carolina pastors and church workers out of more than 700 nationwide accused of sexual improprieties with minors on the once-secret list recently made public by the Southern Baptist Convention.

To read the summaries is to be sickened by a litany of lewd and lascivious acts performed on children by men who were trusted to be saintly.

As those who've followed the story know, the incidents are

all the more sordid because the SBC did its best to keep them quiet; to explain away the accusations; or, in some cases, to blame the victims. Young men and women with little agency to challenge trusted authorities *but abundant courage to do so* were belittled, disbelieved and disavowed. Sometimes by their own family members.

Following an independent investigation authorized by the SBC, the world's largest Baptist group, it has vowed to reform itself, correct these transgressions and take steps to prevent future occurrences.

I've been pondering the shameful story since it first broke and comparing its revelations to similar situations in my own background, growing up in a fundamentalist Christian church and attending a conservative Christian college. I'm sure others have been, too. It's not pleasant.

The SBC list mentions no Piedmont Triad pastors, but we know that such crimes occur here. Earlier this year, former Forsyth County minister T. Elliott Welch, who blamed stress, anxiety and COVID isolation for his habit of downloading child pornography, was sentenced to a minimum of one year, seven months and a maximum of six years, 11 months, in prison. Once released, he'll have to register as a sex offender for a period of 30 years.

On Wednesday, Jason Wesley Keller, a Davidson County pastor, was convicted of six counts of felonious sexual offense with a student and two counts of taking indecent liberties with a student.

Think about those who get away with such crimes, either because their flocks believe their denials or because their victims are too afraid to speak up.

For several years I've also been following the stories of people who are part of what's called the "exvangelical movement" — people who have abandoned their fundamentalist churches and, in many instances, their faith, because of some distortion between dogma and conscience or intellect. Many of them have shared, via social media, stories of abuse — stories that they also once shared with church authorities who ignored or denied them.

As the SBC victims can attest, such betrayal leaves scars.

I can't help wondering about the patriarchal authority

that makes some pastors all but bulletproof in the face of such accusations. Are these isolated incidents performed by sick and twisted individuals, abetted by weak church leaders afraid to confront controversy? Or are they enabled by their denominations' theological culture, with an emphasis on submitting to authority? Worse, could the attitudes that allow such behavior be intrinsic to the Christian religion itself?

Or to religion itself—in all fairness, Christianity doesn't have a monopoly on leaders who are guilty of sexual impropriety. Name the religion; it has its abusers.

On the other hand, can anyone name a single North Carolina transgender person who's been convicted of a sex crime involving a minor in the last . . . ever?

In an hour-long online search, I found one. *Uno.*

This being Pride month, I can't help but think about all of this in relation to the past and current Republican obsession with the LGBTQ community — recently expressed in our state's watered-down version of Florida's "don't say gay" bill. It's sitting on House Speaker Tim Moore's desk, where he's apparently got the good sense to leave it. I can't help but think about the recurring attempts among Republicans to limit LGBTQ rights, even while still trying to make "gay" and "transgender" synonymous with "pedophile."

They're on the lookout, you see, for gay indoctrination. Never mind the straight indoctrination our children are exposed to via every fairy tale from Cinderella to Snow White. Never mind the conservative Christian indoctrination many of them will sit through for an hour or two this morning and every Sunday morning. It's not the powerful and influential church pastors they want us to worry about — it's those men wearing dresses.

On June 10, Amy Schneider, the first transgender contestant on "Jeopardy!" to participate in the Tournament of Champions, was invited to throw out the ceremonial first pitch in the Giants vs. Dodgers game at Oracle Park. You wouldn't have known that if you'd watched the game report on Fox Sports, which cut to commercial during her pitch, then returned to repeat NASCAR driver Kurt Busch's first pitch from the previous Thursday's game.

That was unintentional, Fox later claimed.

Last month, NC Policy Watch's Joe Killian wrote about the invocation at the recent convention of the Wake County Republican Party:

"Our public education system is in shambles and our children have now become expendable," John Amanchukwu, a youth pastor from Raleigh, told the crowd. "They are being taught that Heather has two mommies and Jodie has two daddies. Our children are being taught to hate our country and hate our flag."

Here's the thing: Some kids *do* have two mommies. Some have two daddies. It's not Amanchukwu's decision to make. And there's not a damn thing he can do about it, except groom his children to hate them.

But if you want to make a kid hate America, do this: Wrap yourself in the flag, then tell him that the people who feed him, protect him and take care of him when he's sick aren't his *real* parents. Rip him away from those people and give him to strangers in the name of your country.

That should do it.

As I write this on Friday, the Forsyth County Republican Men's Club is preparing to protest against the Drag Queen Story Time scheduled for Saturday morning at Bookmarks downtown, where the magical, glittery Anna Yacht will read — will have read, by now — stories of unicorns to kids who just like good stories.

I guess the Southern Baptist Convention headquarters in Nashville, Tenn., is a little too far for a day trip.

I don't expect much to have happened; maybe a few raised voices. I do suspect the Republicans' real purpose is to provoke some "You wouldn't believe what those gay people yelled at us!" stories with which to raise funds and votes.

And tempers.

Just like some trusted church pastors, some Republican officials have decided to exploit young, vulnerable people for their own gain.

They're more concerned that your children might discover that gay people exist — and be OK with that — than they are that the kiddie-porn addicted pastor they see three times a week might have an opportunity to be alone with them.

Stop. Taking. The. Bait.

Hid in the clouded wrath of the crowd

Aug 21, 2022

It finally happened — and in red-state Texas of all places. If it can happen in that conservative bastion, it can happen anywhere.

Last week, the Keller Independent School District in Texas pulled the Bible — all versions — from its school library shelves.

"I told you this was going to happen," former Fox contributor Todd Starnes said on his radio show on Wednesday. "I told you they were going to come after the Bible."

What Starnes didn't say, though, was that "they" weren't wild-eyed liberal secularists who hate America, but Keller parents and community members who didn't want their children — or anyone else's children — to read "inappropriate" books. They've challenged 41 titles in the Keller school system since October, which will undergo review before being "canceled" or returned to the library shelves. They include a graphic novel adaptation of "Anne Frank's Diary" and Toni Morrison's "The Bluest Eye" — books about minority, marginalized people.

In all truth, the Bible was likely added to the list by a parent who thought this would be a good opportunity to make a pertinent point. As I write, the Bibles are likely already back in their places.

But conservatives were the ones "going after" books. The Bible just got caught in the crossfire.

It could happen again, though, in earnest, perhaps even successfully, given the unquestionably graphic and sexually explicit material in the Bible.

To read the Bible for one's self is to discover a complex collection of writings that include sublime poetry, thunderous prophetic visions and pensive philosophy.

But it also includes episodes that never make it to Sunday school — especially not in classes for children. There are too many depictions of depravity: rape, murder and incest; whoring and thievery; endless human exploitation; body dismemberment, bloodthirsty revenge and torture. To seek child-like wholesomeness from the Bible one must wrestle with a God who says, "Thou shalt not murder" — except for witches, disobedient children, fidgeters who work on Saturday and foreigners who live on land that God wants his followers to have. Murder them.

It's to deal with phrases like "genitals as large as a donkey's and emissions like those of a horse" and the nature and personality of King Saul's son Jonathan, whose love for the shepherd David "surpassed the love of women." It's to wonder why, when his followers conquered new lands, God instructed them to kill everyone except the young virgins, whom they were to keep for themselves.

Incidentally, anyone who insists that God commands that you should never alter your physical body must explain circumcision to me.

If the real problem that parents want to confront is exposure to explicit or confusing information for which children are not prepared, then the Bible — at least parts of it — must be included in the prohibitions.

But that won't happen, of course. Not because its gruesomeness is in some way different from that in a Stephen King novel, but because the Bible is a cultural sacred cow. To challenge anyone's access to it is to risk the ire of many who revere it despite never having read it.

And also because "inappropriate" is not really what they're after.

State legislative proposals to restrict the freedom to teach and learn have increased by 250% in 2022 compared to 2021, according to a report released last week by PEN America. Some 60% of the bills focus on race and LGBTQ issues in K-12 education.

Those books challenge conservatives' vision of a straight, white-majority Christian America.

Following recent criticism — including from this newspaper — trustees of UNC-Chapel Hill in July adopted a resolution "reaffirming the university's longtime commitment to academic freedom — a principle doubted in some quarters of American society and attacked in others, but vital to all." They concluded: "A university, if it is to be true to its faith in intellectual inquiry, must embrace, be hospitable to, and encourage the widest diversity of views within its own community."

The same should be true for all schools, all libraries.

Children will be drawn to what they need to know. That may include books that explain racism or transgenderism. With mental health challenges reaching epidemic levels among teens, such books could save their lives.

Such books could also save them from the oppressive directives of religious zealots who seek to restrict their knowledge — and their freedom.

And if the lights are all down

Aug 28, 2022

Acorns have been falling on our heads at Fox-a-Lago, the field near Washington Park where my friend and I go daily to watch wild red foxes scamper and play. I've wondered if the barrage might signify an early fall, but the temperature reminds me that the end of August is never the end of warm weather in these parts. Give it a couple of months.

A walk into the woods by the field, though, is a walk into a different world, with a shift toward coolness and a shadowy color scheme.

It was the foxes that first led us here, but they're only a part of this urban wildlife refuge. We've seen deer, raccoons, wild turkeys, owls, an obstinate groundhog and scads of crows. We've also captured, on the trailcams we placed in the woods, an opossum we call The Opossum Paul, as well as stray dogs and stray people.

But recently, things have changed. The fox I came to know as Blondie — named by the grandchildren of a previous observer — hasn't appeared since the end of July. The other foxes have been missing for about as long, even from trailcam footage. It's as if they all up and left.

Foxes can change their territory, an N.C. Wildlife Resources

Commission rep told me, for any number of reasons. They might be chased away by coyotes (which we've never seen, not one). They might just find another place they like better, with more voles and fewer raccoons (which compete with them for food).

It's not unusual for Blondie to skip a day or even a week now and then — wild animals are unpredictable — but it's been too long now. It's hard not to imagine the worst. Wild foxes die from disease and parasites, from fights with other animals, from being hit by cars. Rarely from old age.

A couple of raccoons have stumbled in often enough to receive their own names: Francois and Isabelle. We chuckle as they chase each other around.

But they're not Blondie.

I first saw Blondie, the most petite of all the foxes at Fox-a-Lago, about two years ago. She always looked wary and alert — perhaps, I thought, the result of growing up as a runt, having to fight for her place in the leash and her right to the forest's bounty. At first she hung back in the woods with the younger kits while her mom, Red, came tramping out to see who we were. After Red vanished last year, Blondie grew bolder and claimed her new role as the Matriarch of the Meadow. Over time, she's come closer and closer to me, on occasion sitting nearby, sharing the quiet. Sometimes she'd be waiting for me when I arrived. I felt she trusted me — as much as a wild thing can trust an intruder.

I trusted her, too, never once fearing her sharp teeth and claws.

An acquaintance, artist Kathy Fosselman, captured her facial expression in a painting she gave me. She also caught Blondie's expressive tail; she was the rare red fox whose tail had a dark tip rather than white.

Blondie could be, by turns, energetic and contemplative; hesitant and exuberant. Foxes have their own personalities, like anyone else. I've seen some who were very gentle around their people and others who were spunky and mischievous. I've read that their anatomy doesn't allow them to truly smile — they don't have the requisite muscles — but I've seen so many that *seem* to, with the rest of their faces matching the attitude, that I can't help believing that they feel and express delight.

And, sometimes, sadness.

Back in May, a fellow fox enthusiast wrote about a fox she knows:

I know he isn't my fox. I know it's a huge privilege when he comes to visit us. I know he is a wild animal who lives free. I know I love him. I know I feel sad when he doesn't come to visit. I know I hate seeing him when he is injured. I know one day it will come to an end.
White Tail, we love you. I hope you know.

Is it possible that tears came to my eyes when I realized that my time with Blondie might have reached its end?

Yes, it is.

One day last week, thinking the trailcams might not be working properly, we replaced them. The next day, we recovered a 10-second recording with about two seconds of a familiar face: Scalawag, the fox we saved from death by treating his mange. He returned the next night, followed by a new fox, one we'd never seen before, with a beautiful, thick brush that had a glowing white tip.

We'll keep watching, knowing that it could end any day.

The slow parade of fears

Oct 9, 2022

Last weekend, anticipating Halloween, I attended the Wreak Havoc Horror Film Festival at Marketplace Cinemas. It's a little-known and underrated showcase for little-known, underrated films, many of them short, several of them amateur, homemade productions, imbued with dark humor and surprise endings.

Fun was had.

Several of the films repeated the common horror trope of the frightened victim calling to the dark, "OK, come on out now. This isn't funny," in hopes of coaxing a possible act of predatory stalking to resolve itself into a harmless prank. But rather than a friend with questionable taste leaping out with a laugh, most victims were met by deranged killers carrying deadly implements.

Saying, "OK, come on out now. This isn't funny," doesn't seem to work in the real world, either. It doesn't work in Ukraine, where the clumsy but merciless Russian invasion has left a trail of dead children and its unhinged architect threatens the world with nuclear annihilation.

It doesn't work with natural disasters, like in Florida, where the destruction was exacerbated by our uncontrolled experiment of permeating the air we breathe with carbon.

It doesn't seem to work against the unreasoning extremism posed by a faction of one major political party, aligned with a faction of one major religion, every day drawing a little closer to sanctioning the use of violence to get its way.

The paranoia-fueled 1978 flick "Invasion of the Body Snatchers" mirrors a contemporary problem. Discovering that your mother or your brother has been replaced by an extraterrestrial pod and implanted with unearthly knowledge and deadly malice is something like discovering that your mother or your brother has fallen in with a group of fanatics who believe, *actually believe*, that Tom Hanks is a secret pedophile and John F. Kennedy Jr. faked his 1999 death in order to better fight him — in league with *Donald Trump*, of all people. It's not much of a stretch to say that a significant number of Americans feel a sense of horror as they watch a loved one sink into the QAnon obsession.

Or fall in with Proud Boys. Or Oath Keepers.

But this situation didn't develop overnight.

In 2012, conservative scholars Thomas E. Mann and Norman J. Ornstein warned: "The GOP has become an insurgent outlier in American politics. It is ideologically extreme; scornful of compromise, unmoved by conventional understanding of facts, evidence and science; and dismissive of the legitimacy of its political opposition."

That unconventionality eventually led to a string of stalwart conservatives — Sens. Ted Cruz and Lindsey Graham and former U.N. ambassador Nikki Haley are just a few of the more prominent — seemingly supplanted by pods as their principled opposition to their party's least likely candidate ("Trump is everything we teach our kids not to be," Haley once said) was transformed into groveling servitude.

It also led to then-presidential counselor Kellyanne Conway's promotion, in 2017, of "alternative facts" to assert that the new president's inaugural crowd was larger than it actually was.

Further "alternative facts" proliferated over the next four years, eventually fueling the Big Lie of 2020 election fraud, the "legitimate political discourse" of the Jan. 6, 2021, Capitol attack, liberal "groomers," "furries" in schools who demand access to litter boxes and the distortion of CRT, SEL and other conventionally understood acronyms (in the academic world) into secret socialist plots to make white children hate themselves.

That unconventionality now threatens to undermine and extend violence into the 2022 elections.

OK, come on out now. This isn't funny.

Just like Donald Sutherland and Jeff Goldblum's "Invasion" characters, many uninfected have stepped forward to try to stop the epidemic. They include media commentators Bill Kristol and Matthew Sheffield; former Reps. Joe Scarborough, Joe Walsh and Will Hurd; current Reps. Liz Cheney and Adam Kinzinger; evangelical scholar David French; former Naval War College instructor Tom Nichols; newspaper columnists Max Boot and Jennifer Rubin and former Fox News broadcaster Major Garrett.

These and many others are all trying to warn their fellow conservatives: The signal is coming from inside the house.

The end of this story has not yet been written.

Then you find you're back in Vegas

Nov 3, 2022

The caller was mad.

By which I mean *angry*.

"Why would you put such an ignorant cartoon — here at Thanksgiving — with the Republican and the turkeys?" he asked in his message, left on my office phone a couple weeks ago.

You remember the cartoon? It depicted an elephant dressed as a pilgrim, moving toward an ax after marking two turkeys — one "Social Security," the other, "Medicare."

"You know it's a lie," the caller continued. "They've never said anything about cutting Social Security or Medicare. You're just a damn propaganda arm for the damn Democrat (sic) Party."

Oh, friend, if only that were true.

Of course, neither the Journal nor the cartoonist, the Atlanta Journal-Constitution's Mike Luckovich, plucked the topic out of thin air. Let's go to the videotape, Warner.

As people who follow the news will know, this has become a legitimate topic for discussion — and satire — because of Florida Sen. Rick Scott's 11-point plan to "Rescue America." Among his proposals are "sunsetting" — ending automatically — all federal programs after five years. That would include Social Security and Medicare.

Of course, Scott insisted later, repeatedly, on cable TV, that's not what he meant.

It's just what his proposal says. In writing.

I admit that I was shocked when Scott — no relation, I promise — first introduced the idea, especially during an election season. It seems a strategy that might lead the rank-and-file to think, *that Democrat candidate doesn't look so bad after all.*

The problem is that too many will be like my caller friend: *They'd never do that. That's just fake news.*

They'll say that all the way to the food bank.

They'll say that as other Republicans pick up the ball and run with it.

They include Don Bolduc, a New Hampshire GOP Senate nominee, who in August said it was "hugely important" to privatize Medicare — only to rescind his remarks a day later and offer unequivocal support for Medicare, Medicaid and Social Security.

They include Wisconsin Sen. Ron Johnson, who also in August on "The Regular Joe Show" said it was a problem that Social Security and Medicare were "mandatory spending." He suggested switching the earned benefit programs to discretionary spending, which would be reviewed annually.

And cut at Congress' will.

The Congress that Republicans plan to run.

Of course, not all Republican legislators are on board with the idea. The savviest of them, Senate Minority Leader Mitch McConnell, responding to Scott's plan, said, "We will not have as part of our agenda a bill that raises taxes on half the American people and sunsets Social Security and Medicare within five years."

But the same McConnell also promised, after passing the $1 trillion Trump tax cuts in 2017, to make up the difference by cutting Medicare and Social Security.

All of this is well documented.

Last month, Bloomberg Government interviewed four Republican legislators who all hope to serve as chair of the House budget committee next year. Each one signaled that he would use the debt ceiling as a point of leverage to force Democrats to accept concessions and reductions to Social Security and Medicare.

All of those Republicans would likely claim — as Republican legislators have often claimed — that they want to save and protect our earned benefits.

But somehow saving these programs always involves *reducing* their provisions. To get an increase, like the 8% increase expected in 2023, you need Democrats.

On some level, social spending will always be incompatible with conservative ideology. Social Security is a "socialist" program, after all. It's right there in the name.

And it's one that *works*. It allows the elderly to live their golden years with some degree of dignity and security rather than perish in the kind of poverty and despair that had previously been the norm for too many.

That has to be embarrassing for a party that insists the federal government can't do anything right.

It also puts our money in a safe place where profiteers can't reach it or risk it. That's got to chafe some rich campaign donors.

Maybe I'm wrong. I can be fooled — a principle I always have to consider.

So don't take my word for it. Get on Google and do your own research.

And decide how much of your future you're willing to risk — to the people who are willing to risk yours.

While the clock keeps the pace

Nov 6, 2022

One of my earliest memories is of a birthday party.

I don't remember how old the girl across the street was — the first girl I ever kissed — but I was 4 or 5.

Mom dressed me in a tiny blue suit with a white shirt and yellow bow tie. She combed my short hair.

I must have been a cutie.

"Be sure to say 'thank you,'" she drilled into me, repeatedly.

I ran over to the party and found myself surrounded by a bunch of kids. It was exciting!

The first thing we did was play "pin the tail on the donkey." Amazingly enough, I won. (Amazingly enough, I felt this exhibited some real talent on my part.)

I was given a prize — I've long forgotten what. But after receiving it, I said to the grown-ups present, "Thank you, I had a nice time. I'm going home now."

"Wait!" some tall person yelled after me as I ran across the street. "We're just getting started. There's going to be ice cream and cake!"

"I don't want any," I called back. "Thank you!"

Mom was equally surprised by my behavior, but I felt confident in my decision. I knew that if I stayed at the party, some other kid would try to steal my prize.

Looking back now, I laugh — and sigh, at a decision that seemed so rational at the time and so childish today. I could have had ice cream and cake, which far outweighed any game prize I hoarded.

That memory came to me recently, almost as if it was a piece that finally fit in a confusing mental puzzle.

For years, I've wondered why people of a conservative mindset — some of whom I like very much — vote so consistently not only against their own self-interests — against policies that would provide them and theirs with better and less expensive health care, more resources for public schools, etc. — but also against other people's well-being. They're unmoved by stories of the suffering of poor people, of women and even of refugees who bring their children here to escape torture and murder. Why are they so often focused on protecting what they have rather than seeking improvement for everyone?

I ask this against the backdrop of American history: the Wilmington insurrection of 1898, when white people, feeling threatened by the economic progress of Black people, ginned up excuses to commit theft and murder rather than simply allow them to be prosperous.

The same happened in Tulsa, Okla., in 1921, resulting in the injury of thousands of Black residents and the deaths of up to 300.

In Prince Edward County, Va., following the Brown v. Board of Education decision in 1954, government officials *closed all public schools* rather than allow them to be integrated. For five years, the only education available to any (white) child was through private schools.

In Montgomery, Ala., St. Louis, Mo., and hundreds of other cities in the 1940s and '50s, rather than allow Black kids to swim with white kids in integrated public swimming pools, local governments closed and even filled in the pools — so not even white kids had a place to go swimming.

There's a fear that infects — not all, but many white conservatives and leads them to poison the well for everyone. How absurd is it for people at the top of the food chain, with every advantage our society affords, to feel like they're being cheated when they hear "Black Lives Matter"? What is that except some raw and unreasonable insecurity?

Some say this explains why the U.S. is the only industrialized nation that doesn't have universal, affordable health care. Some white folks would rather their own kids lack coverage than pay any part of Black folks' medical bills.

Is that selfish fear reflected at all in the GOP candidates who won't promise to abide by 2022 electoral results? Is it reflected in Wisconsin gubernatorial candidate Tim Michels, who said last week that if he's elected, "Republicans will never lose another election in Wisconsin"? It's hard not to think so.

Maybe those of us who work for, hope for, what we loosely call "progress" or even "enlightenment" have been taking the wrong tack. Maybe rather than trying to reason with such people, we should have been trying to gently reassure them: *No, it's OK, we still see you. Of course you still matter. We won't take anything from you.*

Maybe it bears constant repetition.

I realize I'm writing about conservative-minded people as if they're not reading this. But I hope you are, friends. I know you want to be good and righteous people.

But the voices that tell you that other people's success takes something from you are lying. Their hatred and anger will twist your good will. They will, ultimately, leave you scrambling for a prize that's worth nothing.

Through eyes that only see what's real

Nov 20, 2022

Most of the leaves have fallen at Fox-a-Lago, the field near Washington Park where a friend and I keep an eye on wild red foxes as they scamper and play. The leaves have created a crisp and thick carpet that allows us to hear the foxes' steps, which would otherwise be stealthy. The colors — bright yellows, reds and rusts — carry an air of stained glass and sometimes the field, bordered by trees 90-feet tall or more, feels like a cathedral.

The cast has changed once again, as happens for reasons unknown. We're now most likely to see Egbert, a mature dog fox with a tail that turns sharply down at its end; Tiny, a teenager (in fox years) with a face that carries an expression of naïve innocence; and a third that hasn't yet shown often enough to receive her own name.

Tiny first appeared with evident signs of the mange that afflicted an earlier cadre, so we've been treating the whole bunch. It seems to be working, but the sun is so low when they arrive that we can't get the clear visual confirmation we'd prefer. The trailcams need replacing, perhaps at next payday.

My friend and I watch the foxes come forth, in a run or a gentle, carefree lope, sometimes hopping like bunnies over successive clumps of tall grass, sometimes dashing past each other or pulling their ears back as they bray some untranslatable message. Though we're keeping a decent distance to avoid scaring them off, they're aware of our presence and it seems not to bother them much.

"What are they thinking?" we regularly ask each other. We'll never know. We'll never stop asking.

Late last month I joined another friend, artist Lynn Byrd, to visit another type of shrine: the little pet chapels she's responsible for in three local parks: Long Creek, Miller, and the Muddy Creek greenway. Each one is something like a little free library, but inside their solid wooden doors, people find art supplies — paper, colored pens, etc. — on which they can scribble a remembrance of the pets they've known and loved; the explorers, protectors, comedians and confidantes who brought them joy, who supported them, sometimes through hard times. Lynn's capable husband, Jamie Cheshire, builds them. Lynn paints them in her exuberant, colorful style. County workers install them. Then people find them and fill them with messages:

"Foz was the most gentle, loving boy. I miss him every day."

"You were so loved Desmond."

"Forever loved and missed, Palomito."

They leave photos: Boo, a stout, sober-looking white dog with black patches; Coconut, a wise black and yellow cat with white paws. At the Miller Park chapel, I left a little picture I drew of Blondie, the fox I loved best, who disappeared toward the end of July.

Wednesday marks one of my favorite holidays: Wolfenoot. Founded by a little boy who lives in New Zealand, it honors canids — dogs, wolfs, foxes — and the people who are kind to them. (I'm sure that cats could be considered honorary canids for a day.) "Wolfenoot is about celebrating our pack — human and animal — helping where we can, and making the world a better, kinder place," says the official Wolfenoot website. Some other holiday occurs later in the week, perhaps riding on Wolfenoot's coattails, but I've ordered my Wolfenoot cake and there will be, at Mick's den, gifts and some enthusiastic if lame howling.

There are wildlife rehabbers and sanctuary owners whose

interventions to help injured or abandoned foxes and other animals far surpass my efforts.

There are so many people whose dedication to their pets fills their lives with love and comfort. It's an unparalleled accomplishment, to give a dog or a cat a happy life.

I often imagine having my own furry companion. It's a pleasant thought, and a goal for . . . someday. Someday when there's room enough, time enough, in my hectic life.

As an editorial writer, I regularly encourage people to take furry creatures into their homes — there's a great need in our community to do so.

Some might think me a tad hypocritical, urging others to adopt while not doing so myself.

But here's what some would miss: I *envy* those of you who do adopt. I aspire to be like you. I can't help but acknowledge you and urge others to join you.

I'm among those who think that if there are no dogs in heaven, I ain't going. Wherever they go — these playful, guileless, giving creatures — that's where I want to be.

Happy Wolfenoot.

With two cats in the yard

Dec 18, 2022

The trees are bare at Fox-a-Lago, the field near Washington Park where a friend and I go to watch wild red foxes play, so we can peer deep into the woods. I stand at their edge, softening and widening my gaze as Dave Hall, the author of "The Naturalist's Companion," suggests, hoping to catch movement, a flash of red, in the distance.

But we usually see little until we sit still and they come to us.

It's getting cold now, and wet, but we've just finished a 10-week course of treatment for Tiny's mange and we want to see her eager, furry face. So we wait. Eventually she arrives, running the path she's worn in the grass and looking over her shoulder to see if we're chasing her. We're not.

Egbert stops and glares at us sometimes, whether with fondness or disgust, we just don't know. Certainly not fear, not at this point.

The third resident, with the bushiest tail, is still too shy and scarce to tell us her name.

Sometimes we hear them, back in the woods, squabbling, but they're too polite to do it in front of us.

Their coats, thickening with cooler temperatures, are now not just beautiful, but practical. Contrary to popular belief, they only go to den when they're hiding or preparing to give birth. They live and sleep outside in the territory they've claimed as home, brushes wrapped around their bodies.

Deer also show up regularly to Fox-a-Lago, one with a very impressive set of antlers. Francois the raccoon sneaks out on occasion, as do two stray cats: We call one Chicken; the other, Noodle.

Eventually we retreat, almost shivering, to the car's heater and my friend says, "Heat is *good*." I agree. Heat is a balm. At home, I sit to read with a fleece blanket wrapped around my legs.

A few years ago — a few years before it became necessary for me to buy a house — I came across this photograph of Trappist monk Thomas Merton standing outside his hermitage: a flat-roofed, concrete-block shack in Kentucky that now serves as a pilgrimage site for would-be mystics. Its simplicity, in design and function, immediately appealed to me.

There was also something about it that reminded me of structures I'd seen in Kernersville while growing up.

I sent a JPEG to my friend, the Realtor, and asked, "Can you find me one like this?"

Unfortunately, no; there are no one-room shacks for sale within city limits.

What I finally bought, a small bungalow in the Washington Park neighborhood, exudes a similar air of simplicity. Or so I imagine.

Some might call it rundown. I call it relaxed.

Despite being on the smaller side, it sometimes still feels too big.

The advantage of a studio apartment is that when you lose something, like the bar of handmade soap I bought from a vendor at Cook's Flea Market last weekend, you only have to search one room.

Now there are four. A proper search can take four times as long. But there's room for plenty of books, so. It evens out.

It took nearly two years, but I'm finally beginning to feel at home there. All the walls I wanted to paint are painted and a large portion of the art hung. The peanut butter is in the proper cabinet. I hardly ever stub my toes anymore. It's hard to keep the coffee table clear of clutter, but that's the story of my life.

"Home" carries different meanings for different people. For

some, like me, it's a refuge and a staging site for the next day's travels.

For others, home requires space for companions who provide a comfortable level of conversation and ambient sound, and decorative touches as well as space to entertain guests.

"Home means a future," says a Habitat for Humanity recipient.

Po Chu-i, the ninth-century Chinese poet, wrote of his home in practical terms:

> *A new thatched hall, five spans by three;*
> *Stone steps, cassia pillars, fence of plaited bamboo.*
> *The south eves catch the sun, warm on winter days;*
> *A door to the north lets in breezes, cool in*
> *summer moonlight.*

Mostly, a home needs to provide a sense of safety and security — especially when children live there.

Some lack such homes. They grow up constantly on edge.

And some shiver at night in their cars, or on the streets.

I'm grateful for what I have: a place to rest my head; to burn candles; to stretch my arms; to tell secrets; to read and think and dream.

Until I grow a fur coat and sleep under the moon, this little shanty will do just fine.

A world in white gets underway

Dec 31, 2022

I have so many things to tell you.

I realize that I don't have to squeeze them all in right now just because the year has ended. I'm sure there will be other opportunities to try your patience.

But I imagine I can *feel* the years changing, as if there were an actual door closing between them, cutting off our access to the past. Time doesn't slip away, it runs away. So many of my days have jumped from 7 a.m. to 9 p.m. in a flash.

So I've just got to tell you.

About "Surrender: 40 Songs, One Story," the memoir by U2 front-man Bono, the most extraordinary book I've read in a good decade. I still remember the first time I heard the driving bass line of, appropriately enough, "New Year's Day," in 1983 — their music was like nothing I'd ever heard before. I wasn't even sure this was a rock band, this *U2*, but its energy transformed my unrest into urgency.

Now, 40 years later, "activism" isn't adequate to express Bono's own urgency, standing on the front lines of music, disease and war. Read this damn thing.

About Cody Johnson, the Beulah, Ga., army vet written up last month in The Washington Post, who wouldn't put up with the hateful, endemic ignorance that infected almost everyone around him. He'd been inoculated against it by reading "The Hobbit" and Ralph Waldo Emerson, the American prophet of self-reliance. No wonder some people are trying to censor libraries.

His lesson: There is a different way to be.

About "You know that one girl, Rachel," the Liberty University graduate, TikTok content creator and irreverently witty interpreter of our times, whose stunning mission statement has stuck with me through nights and days:

"Hi, this message is for the older generations of the evangelical church who always told us while we were growing up that you were praying for our generation to rise up and to bring about revival. That — that's what this is. This is revival. We are trying to bring the body of Christ away from harmful things like Christian nationalism, racism, misogyny, bigotry, and bring it back to being about Jesus, his death, resurrection and his teachings.

"This is the revival that you were praying for. And you're calling it heresy."

About the other kids (a "kid" being pretty much anyone younger than me) I noticed this last year, and how hopeful I feel, seeing them rise up against oppression and hypocrisy and cruelty.

The year tossed some things at me, including a bout of COVID and an episode of Lyme disease that left me feeling grouchy and unable to concentrate. I had to accept that Red's daughter, Blondie, would no longer visit us at Fox-a-Lago. And there's no way to replace Sharon Randall, whose final uplifting column we printed yesterday.

But I come out of 2022 feeling light. It could have been so much worse. I didn't have to face government-employed bigots insisting that public libraries should cater only to their beliefs. I didn't have to suffer arrogant legislators forcing me into dangerous situations or acting like they knew me better than my parents, my doctors, my spiritual advisers and me. There was no invading force, practicing institutionally approved murder and rape, determined to destroy my very nationality, aided and abetted by American cable-TV commentators.

Four-dollars-a-gallon gas? Pfft.

I got to pet the heads of lots of dogs. I got to learn about raccoons and opossums. There was this cat that sat on my chest and purred.

I got to hang out in restaurants and movie theaters and on hiking trails with friends who make me laugh. I got to travel to the Inner Banks, to Virginia and south to Eagle Springs to get ice cream.

I got to spend a few sessions with a professional counselor. I'm better for it.

And though I spent so much time feeling rushed, I also got to sit still, pretty much every day, at Fox-a-Lago, the field where the wild red foxes play.

I'm satisfied with 2022.

I don't know what 2023 will bring. But in the field, we're wondering just what the relationship is between Egbert and Tiny. This is the time of year when such matters are defined. We're listening for the unearthly screeches that sometimes indicate a moment of agreement.

You see, when a daddy fox and a mommy fox love each other very much . . .

We're anticipating kits in the springtime, little puffballs of trembling wonder.

And maybe that's a good wish to leave with you now: I hope you have, in 2023, many little puffballs of trembling wonder. Happy New Year.

Freedom's just another word

Jan 15, 2023

"Words have meaning," a friend said to me last week as we discussed issues of the day, and I agree wholeheartedly. It's a gentle reminder — OK, a slightly pointed reminder (words have meaning) that word choice and vocabulary are important and that reality is both nuanced and precise. Not every Republican is a far-right extremist; neither is every Democrat a woke liberal. No, really.

Take "freedom."

Last year, Arizona gubernatorial candidate Kari Lake gave an interview to Liam Bartlett, a reporter with Australia's version of "60 Minutes," in which things got a little heated.

Complaining about the treatment of the alleged insurrectionists who were in prison awaiting trial (like, it must be said, thousands of other criminal suspects, for whom Lake, et. al., have expressed little concern), Lake said, "Maybe they get away with that stuff in Australia. Perhaps in Australia, because you've given your rights away, you've melted down all of your guns and you guys have no freedom, you find that OK."

In the early '80s, I spent a little time abroad, including about a year in Sydney. I don't think about it much these days, but I still remember how surprised I felt at the sight of topless women swimming and sunbathing at Bondi Beach, not far from downtown. I was not accustomed to that degree of personal freedom.

That may be a trivial example. But here's another freedom Australians have that we don't: An Australian can bump into someone on the sidewalk and say, "Why don't you watch where you're going?" without worrying that the clumsy oaf might pull out a gun and shoot him. An Australian can get into a shouting match down at the pub without worrying that some drunk bloke might get a little too carried away and shoot him.

And Australian children can go to school every day without worrying much about someone showing up with an AR-15 to shoot them.

I watched an analysis of Lake's "60 Minutes" interview by an NRA rep who goes by the name Colion Noir, who said: "Regardless of where you stand politically, one thing is true: The only thing that deters governments from overstepping their power and becoming tyrannical is the government realizing that if they go too far, people have the ability to effectively fight back. The Second Amendment is the big-ass bodyguard at the club."

"True" is a word with meaning, and I don't think it applies here. It's not our personal arsenals that keep us free. It's the rule of law; it's our traditions; it's our free press; it's our commitment to fair elections; it's our *civilization.*

And it includes keeping our military free of political influence, as former Defense Secretary Mark Esper and Joint Chiefs of Staff Mark Milley insisted when former President Trump tried to co-opt it to crack down on protesters.

"Tyrannical" is a word with meaning. Who's going to decide whether an administration — or a law, or an election — is tyrannical? People with guns? People with guns who hate it when Democrats are in charge? *They* get to decide?

"Tyrannical" doesn't mean "I don't like Brandon" or "Alex Jones says Italian satellites changed the Dominion machine votes." But those are among the rationalizations that inspired the people who thought Jan. 6, 2021, was their call to arms (in some cases, literally).

The idea that if you don't like an election or a policy or a tax rate, you can just get everyone together and march down to City Hall (or up to Washington) with your guns to set things straight is *insane*. I like people, but in groups, with guns, they can't always be trusted to do what's right — as our history repeatedly attests.

Despite Australians' lack of personal arsenals, no tyrant has ever gained control of their government. People there do like we do: They vote the losers out.

It's the same in pretty much every modern democracy: Japan, France, Norway.

Guns don't, in and of themselves, represent freedom. The assault weapons sported by Proud Boys standing outside drag shows — they represent the threat of murder. Their guns don't say, "Go, do what you want." They say, "If I get the chance, I'm going to kill you."

And "Moms for Liberty" — the group exists to pull books about gender and race off library shelves and keep people from reading them. That's the *opposite* of liberty.

I couldn't complain about "Moms for Vigilance." Well, not about the name. It might be accurate without carrying negative connotations.

But "Moms for Oppression" — those words would be more precise.

Some lace and paper flowers

Mar 21, 2023

A red-tailed hawk appeared in the treetops above Fox-a-Lago last week, perched 100 feet above the field where the red fox we call Sally has reigned for some time now. The hawk peered at the robins and sparrows cleaning up the peanuts below for several minutes before gliding down, magestically, silently, turning up at the last instant to land on empty talons, the expression from her eyes and sharp beak one of vigilance and sobriety.

The other birds scattered.

The hawk, all orange and russet, stepped onto the edge of a plastic bowl we use to hold water, tipping it and spilling the water onto herself, thus breaking her dignified bearing. She flew away humbled.

The next day, her smaller mate replaced her, sitting on a branch not far above a similar-sized crow, feathers gleaming blue-black in the sunlight. We wondered what interaction they might have, but they politely ignored each other. Then Sally meandered out and the birds took the cue to fly away. Sally sat, jazz-age cool, licked a paw and took in her domain.

We assigned the hawks' gender and relationship the same way we do those of the other creatures; a little bit by study, a lot by imagination. For all we know, the one we call Scruffy

Milton could be in a den nursing her kits right now. All of our conclusions are provisional, subject to new information that might demand we alter our assessments. I think that's a pretty good principle for interpreting life.

And its lack, one of the main causes of today's political division. As someone sarcastically summed it up a good decade ago, "I've already made up my mind; don't confuse me with the facts."

A few nights ago I dreamed that I stood on a snow-covered porch, two thickly coated foxes at my feet. I kneeled to be on their level and they padded their paws at me expectantly, as if inviting me to run away with them. Sadly, I woke instead.

The air above my wool blanket was cold. Light filtered dimly through the window, spurring some childhood memory of lying in bed on a snowy day. I lingered, feeling warm and safe. Then it was time to get up; back to the world.

Back to the world, with its unrelenting responsibilities; with its frictions and inconveniences.

Back to the world of drinking coffee with friends, of hiking and Tai Chi classes, of art and poetry, of grilled cheese sandwiches, waterfalls and chirping birds. I've begun thinking of these gifts as *magic* — not in a supernatural sense, but because they lift us from our mundane circumstances.

Because "survival is insufficient," as wise women from Emily St. John Mandel to Seven of Nine have reminded us.

"You need music," Jerry Garcia is said to have said. "I don't know why. It's probably one of those Joseph Campbell questions, why we need ritual. We need magic and bliss, and power and myth, and celebration and religion in our lives and music is a good way to encapsulate a lot of it."

When I left the Journal in the middle of January, I thought that would be the end of my writing career. I'd always written, but with no more deadlines pressing, and other interests beckoning, it seemed a good time to shift my priorities.

But before a month had passed, I'd opened a substack account, where you can find me today if you like.

I've also been participating in local conversations about our need for reliable news sources — *and* the necessity of convincing people to turn from the pleasant-sounding but ultimately empty lies, which teach them to be angry, back to some semblance of reality. That's a tough one — but we've got to find a way or we're doomed.

There's just a whole lot going on. Our nation, our state, our city, face challenges that demand our participation. The decisions we make collectively will define whether we reside in democracy — in freedom and equality — or settle for something less; something stingy and mean; something stilted, discriminatory, selfish and greedy.

I can't ignore the challenges.

I hope you won't, either.

But take the time, as I've resolved to do, for magic. Otherwise, what are we even fighting for?

Winston-Salem native Mick Scott worked in the Winston-Salem Journal's editorial department for 20 years, the final five of those as editorial page editor. During that time, he churned out thousands of editorials and opinion columns on tight deadline and received numerous first- and second-place awards from the North Carolina Press Association. He's lived in four countries and visited 49 of the 50 states. He enjoys travel, reading, making art, and observing wildlife. Follow Mick's current writing at mickscott.substack.com